Afterlife of Animals

This book is dedicated to all animals around the planet, and beyond.

With love and gratitude to Craig Marks and Lisa Lieberman.

Special thanks to Aaron Nash, MS, LMFT; Kim Kmetz, LMFT; Dr. John Roueche, DVM; and Dr. Nicklaus Fox, DVM.

In memory of Seymour, Princess, Chingy, Buster, Justin, Astro, Apache, and Niblet.

Interior and Cover Designer: Darren Samuel
Art Producer: Sara Feinstein
Editor: John Makowski
Production Editor: Andrew Yackira

All photography used under license from Shutterstock.com
Author photo courtesy of © Craig Marks/Cinemedia Studios
Hair and makeup by Julie Lagerwall Riddell

ISBN: Print 978-1-64739-186-7 | eBook 978-1-64739-187-4

R0

AFTERLIFE OF ANIMALS

A Guide to Healing from Loss and Communicating with Your Beloved Pet

CANDI CANE COOPER

ROCKRIDGE
PRESS

Contents

Introduction and How to Use This Book

Losing your animal companion can be one of the hardest chapters in your life. No matter what type of animal you lose, the loss can hit as hard as losing a human companion. Through this book, I will guide you step by step as you embark on your healing journey. I have tried to include all the tools necessary to help you get started. Try to relax and settle in, as you have come to a safe place here with me. Be vulnerable and open, as I'm here to help heal your emotional wounds.

I have worked with the public as a professional interspecies communicator for more than 20 years, and I have acquired a vast knowledge of the afterlife as I visit it just about every day in my work. With a licensed veterinarian, I facilitate physician-assisted euthanasia while also fulfilling the role of a spiritual adviser, sharing animals' last requests, wishes, and thoughts with their human caretakers before they depart, then helping them gently travel across the Rainbow Bridge. My ability to escort animals to the other side has always been my biggest honor.

My client list includes dogs, cats, lizards, snakes, goats, sheep, zebras, squirrels, rabbits, birds, lions, mice, rats, and more. I am a bit different from most communicators because I can actually hear the animal's voice when conversing with them—yes, just like Dr. Dolittle in the movies. Being born with this gift, I have talked to animals my whole life and helped those who can't speak up for themselves. There has never been an animal I could not communicate with, and nothing is left to interpretation or intuition. When in session, my clients and I are having an open conversation in real time. I am only acting as the interpreter, repeating what the animal says as I hear it. This is what I mean when I say, "straight from the communicator's mouth." It's my honor to share the incredible experiences I have had the pleasure of living through with the animals, to aid you on your healing journey.

Before we get started, I want to share one of my most memorable sessions from across the Rainbow Bridge. One of my clients, Rylee, had a beautiful black-and-white male Boxer named Roscoe. Rylee and I worked together since Roscoe was a pup, from housebreaking him to helping him share Rylee's love with his new human baby brother. He was a great dog, always loving and kind to others. After he passed gently at 14 years old, Rylee and I continued to share many sessions together, visiting Roscoe on the other side. Rylee looked to him for spiritual guidance, as he always had a grounding effect on her. She was very curious about what it was like across the Rainbow Bridge, and Roscoe was excited to share with her what his daily adventures there were like.

One day in session, when Rylee was talking to Roscoe about the afterlife, she asked him, "What does it feel like?" He answered, "It feels like I'm everywhere."

I think Roscoe summed it all up with his answer. Yes, our pets are everywhere. The spirit has no boundaries, as the bond between human and animal meshes here and from beyond the Rainbow Bridge.

My one wish is that my book will resonate with you to your core. I hope that you will use the book as a touchstone for years to come, looking back over it time and time again. This is your personal spiritual and healing reference guide, helping you through the grief and mourning and assisting the healing process as you gain an understanding of the animal afterlife.

Crossing the Rainbow Bridge is not an ending but a new beginning. I feel that the Rainbow Bridge is a sacred doorway leading to other dimensions running parallel with ours. Let's take a dive into these secret worlds together, as I share my stories and lessons with you from beyond the Rainbow Bridge.

I wish to open up your mind and motivate you to explore your other senses. I wish to help validate things that you thought were not possible, letting you feel free and safe to look at life and beyond from a different perspective.

Throughout this book, I will be taking you with me to the other side, revealing aspects of the afterlife for you. This will include the most frequently asked questions and most common issues, all filtered from my experience with thousands of clients. Toward the end of the book, I will share different techniques to communicate across the Rainbow Bridge. I will also share an assortment of common signs you may see after your animal is gone, explaining them in depth—including their meanings and how they apply to your everyday life—along with a few simple rituals for you to practice to reach out to your pets and keep them present. I will also explain what the clair senses are so that you can explore them. I have woven a variety of heartfelt stories through each chapter to help you identify with each concept.

For reference, there are a variety of terms I use interchangeably throughout this book. When discussing the afterlife, I use "the other side," "dimension," "zone," "plane," "reality," and "the Rainbow Bridge." I refer to myself as an "animal communicator" or "interspecies communicator." For the animals, I may also use the term "pet." I refer to pet owners simply as "humans" or human "caretakers." I believe that we never own our animals; they are gifts to us for the time we share together.

Though the animal-related stories contained in this book mostly involve canines, felines, and equines, this book applies universally to all animals.

One

ACKNOWLEDGE YOUR GRIEF

The first key to healing and recovery is to simply acknowledge your loss. This can be a difficult step, but it is the most important one during this healing time. Yes, your life has permanently changed, but you will see that the healing process can be achieved. Whether your loss is recent or occurred many years ago, the journey is the same for all.

I want to open this chapter by sharing a short story with you about one of my most treasured clients. If you're currently reading this book, I know you are filled with love and compassion for your pets. So, let's jump in together and share the trials and tribulations we endure for the love of our animals.

My client Lana loved her dog Monty, a chocolate-brown German Shorthaired Pointer, with every fiber of her being. I was certainly bitten by the love bug the moment I met this handsome boy. Hands down, Monty was Lana's entire existence. Unfortunately, he contracted several illnesses that he fought for eight long and hard years. I worked almost daily with this amazing dog, helping him and Lana navigate all the difficulties, including pain management, doctor's visits, and most of all, the emotional endurance that he and his human companion had to muster. Monty fought like Muhammad Ali against all his medical conditions.

Needless to say, it was a lot for all of us. Monty would often page me telepathically late at night or very early in the morning. He would ask me for more medication and a few cookies to help him through the pain. Lana never minded answering a

3 a.m. text or call from me saying Monty needed this or that. She was always there, quietly lying by his side, easing his pain and comforting him until daybreak. Her love surpassed any selfish thoughts we humans may have. Nothing was too hard or unattainable if Monty wanted or needed it. She was his hero, and mine as well.

Following his last stay in the hospital, Monty's physical situation became too much for him to handle. We had our usual weekly session the Saturday night he went home, but later that evening, he paged me on his own. Things had changed for him; he was physically and emotionally spent. He told me that he would never go back to the hospital again—that he was finished with the pain, the hospital visits, and the daily struggle just to survive. He simply asked me to express his thoughts out loud to Lana. My work as a communicator was kicked into high gear, as I had to prepare Lana and Monty emotionally, spiritually, and physically for their new journey together. As I relayed my conversation with Monty to Lana, she went into shock, and we cried together. Even when you have time to prepare yourself for letting your animal go, the reality is extremely hard to absorb. The decision to release Monty was the hardest of Lana's life.

Lana gathered up her courage and told Monty she would set him free. I respected her for her decision to agree to fulfill his wishes and let him go. The next week, Monty was humanely euthanized. I was at home with Lana and the doctor as I escorted

Monty gently and easily across the Rainbow Bridge. Lana had prepared special music for him, and we all sang together. I held on to his paw as he got ready to travel. When the doctor sat down to prepare his injections, Monty walked over and calmly sat right next to him. He looked up at me and said, "I'm ready, let's go"—and so his new journey began.

I guided Lana through this journey as well. Her first step was to acknowledge it, take it in, and feel its heavy weight. Monty's loss would have a rippling effect over everything else in her life. I will share more of Lana and Monty's story through-out this book, and their incredible healing journey together.

You've Suffered a Loss

Some of you may have been lucky enough to spend an entire lifetime with your animal. You've shared all life's daily joys and disappointments together, savoring all the holidays, personal celebrations, and life milestones as one. For some, though, this time was unfortunately cut short. You may have had just a few hours, days, weeks, or months together, but this doesn't change the loving bond that you created with your pet. You have lost a family member—your best friend and confidant. Time and space have no bearing on this loss.

Losing your pet is always a huge shock to your system, whether you anticipated it because your pet had a terminal condition, or extended medical issues, or suffered an accident, or the loss was completely unexpected. The loss will still hit you with the same ravaging effect. Know that the universe has its own plan; you were meant to be in your animal's life for a reason and for exactly just that amount of time. There was nothing you could have done to change that course.

A Beloved Companion

Regardless of what kind of animal your pet was, always remember that your pet's life was just as important to you as that of any family member. There is no need to ever feel embarrassed about your heartache over the passing of an animal.

Adam Clark, LCSW, AASW, wrote in *Psychology Today* that studies have found that "grieving the death of our companion animals can be just as painful, if not more than, grieving the loss of a family member or friend." With this in mind, don't ever feel belittled by anyone who judges you for your reaction to your loss. When you express your grief, some may say, "Just get over it" or "It was just an animal. You're being so dramatic. You'll be okay in a few more days." Maybe your coworkers ask you how you're doing on a daily basis or check in constantly, just to tell you that things will be okay or that you should just relax.

So many of my clients have endured these verbal platitudes after their pet has crossed over. The words can be brutal to hear and think about, especially at this most vulnerable time in your life. You may acknowledge that your coworkers and friends are truly concerned about you, but internally you feel like they're really thinking, "Oh my, when are they going to get over this?" You may feel ashamed and want to run and hide from the empty clichés and endless questioning. However, you must stop reeling from the thoughtless comments that people impose on you. Please remember to be good to yourself; take some time off work, if necessary, and respect your grieving even if others don't. Remember that no one else can possibly feel your pain and no one else has the right to judge you or the effect that grief has on you.

This lack of compassion in the human race can be shocking at times—as a vegan, I'm especially aware of this—but I have also seen humans filled with love and empathy. Look around you and search to find like-minded people. I promise you they exist. Surround yourself with positive, animal-loving beings who feel the same connection to the animal world that you do. This type of support will help you center yourself and realize that you're not alone.

They May Be Gone, but Their Love Isn't

Over time, you might worry that your animal's love for you is slipping away. I can assure you that their spirit stays close and will truly never leave your side. When you're feeling this way, just think about how many times a day they cross your mind, and how everything reminds you of them. Your pet remains deep in your heart and is still a part of your everyday life. You will never lose their love.

Your pet's physical absence is real, so don't try to ignore that fact. Their time in their physical body has expired, and nothing can change that. The knowledge that you can't hold them, pet them, and protect them anymore can bring a new sense of emptiness for you. You may experience feelings of frustration, anger, and isolation over their transition. All these emotions are normal, and you will be okay. When a loved one's spirit leaves the body behind, we tend to feel that it is the end, but as we grow spiritually, we learn that the connection remains. We are all here physically as visitors, because our bodies are not made to last indefinitely.

When working with my clients and their pets on the other side, I always have one small request: I ask that when speaking about their pets to refer to them in the present tense. The reason is that your love does not die or change, and neither does your animal's. The only difference is that now the body is not present in our dimension. Assisting an in-home euthanasia or any situation with an animal crossing over is the most intimate exchange of energy that I have ever experienced. I feel that it's the ultimate honor in my career to be their escort as they transition. The spirit immediately leaves the body and is set free to the afterlife.

The love that you share with your pet is unchanged on all sides. Their love and devotion to you remains the same. Protecting you, guiding you, loving you, bound to you by their passion. Your guardian angel is now watching over you from across the Rainbow Bridge.

Sudden Loss

So many of us lead busy lives, with high demands on our time. We may travel for business, pleasure, or just be out and about for many hours in our daily routines close to home. Our pets are used to dog walkers, in-house pet sitters, day care, and all types of animal facilitators, whom we hire to keep our pets happy, healthy, entertained, and safely out of harm's way while we are away.

But as is the case with all living beings, accidents can happen. Human caretakers all dread the possibility of getting the phone call that their animal is in distress. Your pet may have been gravely injured in an accident. Maybe someone left the side gate open and they ran out confused and got lost. I work with these situations on a daily basis. If your animal has survived but is seriously injured beyond recovery, this can be bittersweet. You are suddenly faced with the hardest decision of your life.

You know in your heart how you must release your pet from the pain, and that euthanizing is the only humane deci-sion. You may also have guilt because you were not there for them. These situations can be emotionally crushing, but if there is ever a time to be totally unselfish, this is it. It's important to stop thinking about the what-ifs and deal with your pet's needs now. Do not let them suffer one moment more than they have to. Everything that you are questioning yourself about will be resolved. Allow me to help show the way to healing and recovery.

As an interspecies communicator, working with lost animals or runaways is one of the hardest things I do. My sessions are not only filled with the animal's anxieties but also those of their human caretakers. When animals are on the run, their survival instincts take over. No animal really wants to be misplaced from his or her home and loved ones. Under these circumstances, they have no control, and this escalates their fears. It is very difficult to know that your best friend is out there somewhere and you may be unable to help them. Their human could be only a few feet away, calling out their name as they search relentlessly, but the lost animal is usually so paralyzed by the situation that they are afraid to come out. Survival is the number one goal for them at such a time. It's a whole different ball game when they are alone in the elements. That's why it's so rewarding when I can reunite a pet with their owner, as the joy felt on both sides is unmatched.

Occasionally, I find a lost pet living in a different home, rescued by a stranger who decided to keep them. Believe it or not, this happens quite often. Even though the pet is not returned, there can be much comfort for the original owner knowing that their pet is safe and well taken care of. In my experience, animals in this situation adapt and eventually fit in nicely with their new human family, although it can be hard for their previous human companion to relinquish them. The alternative for other runaways is not always so pleasant. Being selfless and letting your pet live on is a beautiful gift. I'm grateful when, in this situation, my client can say to their animal, "Please be nice to your new human and show them your love. One day we will see each other again, but for now, be happy and have a wonderful life." The animals always reply with, "I will never forget you, and I will love you forever."

When You Knew It Was Going to Happen

Our animals are always trying to please us, putting our requests at the top of their lists. I ask you to do the same for them, especially when thinking about traveling or leaving your pet for an extended period of time. I will have a straight-up, honest conversation with my clients about traveling if their pet is sick, rehabbing, terminally ill, or just a sweet senior.

I find it amazing how many of you are connected to your sixth sense—that voice you hear deep in your subconscious, or that feeling you get when the hair on the back of your neck rises. Listen to yourself, feel it. You are not imagining it. Don't try to sort it out with conscious rationalization. Sit with the thoughts and take them in. You don't want to feel, deep in the pit of your stomach, that you knew better, thinking after the fact, "Why didn't I listen to myself? This was all avoidable."

There is nothing worse than getting that call we talked about earlier, only this time, you are miles away from your animal. You panic and your mind races, thinking what to do next.

"Can I get a flight out right now? How far is the drive? Will my beloved pet last long enough for me to say goodbye? I don't want them to be scared and alone when they cross over."

Try to be realistic in a situation like this, and weigh all the possibilities before you make travel plans, because it's a hard reality to face when things go wrong. Instead, protect your and your animal's emotional health with just some simple forethought.

I like to have a session with the pet before their human leaves, and ask them their thoughts about being separated from them for a time. Do they need their human there if they feel it's time to transition? Will they feel abandoned? Do they want to be set free now, before they are separated from their human?

These are tough questions, not only to ask but also to hear the answers. Sometimes you just can't avoid leaving your pet, so in that case, always prepare them and yourself. I applaud the courage of my clients who push through their own emotional agenda to prepare for this situation. The truth can be such a comfort, like being swaddled in a warm, soft blanket. When you know you made the best decision for your pet, all the other things that you may have questioned in your mind will magically melt away.

I deal with the aftermath—the guilt of the caretakers who were not prepared. Words cannot express the mental torment of being absent when your animal passes on. I talk in session to many, many pets on the other side that had to transition alone, and the caretakers always ask for their forgiveness. It's just heartbreaking for all when, in most situations, this abandonment could have been avoided.

I know I may sound harsh, but I want to help you sidestep this emotional landmine. The key is to be honest with yourself about your pet's situation at all times, putting them ahead of your own needs and plans.

However, don't ever fear or dread the experience of your pet crossing over, as it can be your most treasured memory together. Even though the animals are aware of the afterlife, I have never spoken with one that wanted to begin the journey alone. Be selfless and put your devoted pet first, as they deserve it. It can be a very cathartic experience to be present when witnessing the spirit leave the body. It brings closure and peace, helping put all things into perspective and setting a balance for you in the universe once again. I work with so many guilt-ridden human caretakers who could not be present for their pet's transition. Don't add any unnecessary emotional distress to your life at this time. Just be present for your pet.

If you have lost a pet and now have or are considering adopting an older pet, I congratulate and applaud you. You have now grown spiritually to the point where you can open your heart to another animal, which is a milestone in your recovery process.

Be prepared and make a succession plan for them. Have medical insurance in place or a separate fund for medical care and expenses. Always plan ahead for unexpected emergencies. Include friends and relatives who can help and step in immediately when you are away. Being proactive can save you from a lifetime of second-guessing yourself.

I have a succession plan for all my animals with my estate attorney. I have a sanctuary lined up to take care of my animals when I cross over, and a savings account for their new caretakers to use for their care and needs after I'm gone. You owe these preparations to them and to yourself. It will bring you great peace of mind to know that you have a secure plan in place for their future.

My goal with this book is to help you manage your loss and help you understand and accept this new chapter in your life. I speak from my heart: Making peace with losing your pet is a struggle, but it can be done, and you will live to love another animal again.

Different Ways of Grieving

My clients through the years have expressed their grief in many different ways. One keeps her dog's collar on her pillow at night when she gets ready for bed. This way, she feels as though he is still with her, and she can still smell his presence next to her. Another client pretends that her loyal dog still goes everywhere with her in the car during her daily routine. She opens the car door for him, puts his blanket down on the seat, secures him into the car harness, and talks to him as she drives. Another client occasionally sleeps in her Great Dane's bed, which brings her comfort when she can't sleep. She holds on to his favorite toy as she imagines him curled up next to her. Some clients take a bit of their animal's ashes to fill a pendant or locket. My clients with larger animals take a portion of the hair from their mane and/or tail and braid it into a bracelet, a necklace, or key chain. You may want to make a keepsake out of anything associated with your pet that means something to you. Be creative and make the souvenir out of whatever makes you feel the closest to your beloved animal.

Allow Yourself to Grieve

Take this time now to look inward and grieve, and try to let all your thoughts wash over and through you.

Here is a simple exercise to get started:

Close your eyes and picture yourself standing on the seashore with your toes in the sand. As the tide comes in and bubbles up around your feet, you feel invigorated and refreshed. Let yourself feel infused with love and gratitude from the ocean. Feel it moving through your toes and up to the top of your head. As the tide starts to flow out, push all your negative thoughts down, back through the bottom of your heels, releasing all negativity into the sea. Don't forget to breathe in as you receive and breathe out as you release.

Take it slow as you sit with your emotions. Never feel any pressure to spring right back into life's daily routines. Your life has changed and will continue to be different. This is your time to adjust. Dealing with grief can take many shapes and appear in many different ways—some big, and some so small that you may not even notice. You may feel scared or disoriented at times. You may cry for no reason. You may lose sleep and your appetite, or experience fits of anger and outbursts of frustration. You may have feelings of sheer hopelessness, guilt, and loneliness. These are just a few examples of how grief can be expressed or experienced.

Let me reiterate: All this is normal. It is crucial to be honest with yourself and your feelings now. There is no "right way" to feel, so try to relax and let the emotions pass through you. Don't pretend to be strong, don't stop yourself from crying when you need to, and don't force thoughts out of your head. Take them in, acknowledge them, then let them work their way through your system naturally.

Trying to ignore your grief or pushing it down and away will not make it pass any faster. There is no time limit on the grieving process. The hole you have in your heart and soul is real, so please find comfort that I know, see, and feel all your pain. We have all experienced these emotions when we have suffered a loss like this.

Do you feel that you may be suffering from depression? Grief and depression are two different issues but often go hand in hand. If you feel you need support from a mental health professional, please seek that out and find help from a therapist or another licensed mental health professional who is like-minded about animals.

Talking, talking, and more talking is cathartic. Talking about your feelings is an opportunity to mend. The more you express and share, the faster you can reclaim a balance in your life. I have many sessions every week with clients just to connect with their animals on the other side. It's very emotionally soothing for them and their pets to be able to talk after the pets have crossed over. We usually start our communication from when they first passed over, to what they are doing today across the Rainbow Bridge.

Now let's discuss the healing process.

Straight from the communicator's mouth: Only when you have accepted all your pain can you allow healing to begin.

Two

START TO HEAL

As we move into our discussion of the healing process, let me share more with you about Lana and Monty's journey. Months after she released Monty across the Rainbow Bridge, Lana still didn't believe that she would survive his loss. Her entire day had centered completely on him, including what time to wake up, when to administer his meds, day care, walking, play-dates, car rides, the park, grooming, and those endless doctor appointments—not to mention all his emotional needs.

Lana has coped with the aftermath the best that she can. Dealing with the loss of Monty remains a day-by-day process for her—some days are okay, and others are very hard—and I have been working on it with her since his departure. She has talked with Monty through me the whole time, checking in on him and his adventures in his new world. As they share their days together again in session, all is perfect in her world again.

I do feel she is on the topside of things now. I can say that after 11 months, Lana finally feels like she can let herself start to heal. Personally, I am so happy that her constant question-ing of her past actions and what-ifs—Did he have a good life here? Did I keep him pain-free? Did I do the right thing letting him go?—has dissipated. She now feels that she did all that she could and all the right things for Monty.

You may wonder how long it will take before you can think about feeling better, but no matter how much you plan, there is no set time frame for recovery. Be gentle with yourself and let nature take its course. The universe wants you to be happy and has a plan just for you.

Healing Is a Process

You might be thinking, "Candi, I'm not ready yet. It's just too soon." Just try to relax, as it's my purpose here to gently guide you along this process. Never feel that something is wrong with you or that you are "wired incorrectly." You're no different from anyone else navigating these very same emotions. For so many of us, our animals are not just our best friends but our whole world. I have thousands of clients around the world who feel this way. I respect and share this deep connection to our animals.

One Day at a Time

No matter how long your pet has been gone, you need to address your emotions and let them out, as long as they're not destructive. Keeping your emotions inside will only be detrimental. Don't be embarrassed if waves of emotion overwhelm you in public. Express your sadness in the moment when it overtakes you, then examine it, own it, and once again release whatever feelings you have. This is a healthy, normal process for your healing phase. Try also to share these emotions with like-minded friends and family when you can. Now is the time to lean on others—whether it is just one friend, your therapist, an animal communicator, or a support group of caring individuals. Sometimes, it does take a village.

It's Okay to Have Feelings!

It's common to feel that others will unintentionally pick at your fresh emotional wounds while trying to help or expressing interest in your plight. Your first instinct may be to be polite, smile, and say thank you, when inside you want to burst into tears.

You may be thinking how just this morning it was so hard to wake up without your soul mate, how the pain in your stomach is so strong you can barely make small talk with these individuals. You want to shout out, "I just lost the love of my life, my heart animal. My heart is broken in two, and I feel that I may never recover." Doesn't this sound more like the conversation you really want to have? Most people feel very uncomfortable discussing death, so they express some common niceties and move on, feeling that they have fulfilled their social obligation, but in reality they have shown you no comfort or compassion at all. My best advice is to always be honest in these situations and let it out. This is your life, your journey, and you have the right to express your true feelings even when others gloss over them.

Talk to Others

When leaning on your support group and expressing your emotions, you can use the opportunity to educate the less enlightened about our animal brothers and sisters. Gather your strength in the moment and respond from your heart. Let them know that many of us love and cherish our animals with the same conviction as we love and cherish our human counterparts. Let them see the empathy in your eyes and feel your deep compassion. Openly addressing your thoughts and feelings is an opportunity for you to show others the ways of a true animal lover. Turn this into a positive experience for you as you continue to heal, showing your respect for the animals at the same time.

Help Your Other Pets through Their Grief

Helping your remaining pets to cope with this loss is a must, as they also need time to heal. Being there for them now is more important than ever. I have seen so many animals grieve their friend's loss, as it's just as heartbreaking for them as it is for us. All animals grieve when they lose their companions, and they can show their grief in many different ways.

One of my clients lost her beloved horse of 25 years, Miracle, a beautiful red sorrel Arabian mare. Miracle's companion was Dante, a black Half Quarter Horse Mustang gelding, and their love was unmatched. Miracle's owner, Jennifer, wanted to keep her close after her passing, so Miracle was buried in the backyard. A few days later, Jennifer noticed some strange markings on the dirt where Miracle rested in peace. A week later, Jennifer was sitting out by the window late in the evening and she couldn't believe her eyes: Dante was sleeping on top of Miracle's grave. How incredibly touching to see him grieving his loss and wanting to be as close to her as possible. He found great comfort in sleeping there, as it was literally as close as he could get to Miracle since she crossed the Rainbow Bridge. He continued to sleep on top of Miracle's grave every night until his passing a few years later. They are now reunited across the Rainbow Bridge.

I have another client who lost her cat, Felix, when he was 21 years old. Felix was a strong, hearty orange tabby with bright green eyes. His other animal family consisted of three female cats and one male dog. The dog was a large Rottweiler named Poindexter. Poindexter tolerated the other three cats, but he and Felix were best friends. One late night, Felix had some serious medical complications and had to be rushed to the emergency room. He unfortunately didn't survive and never came home. For the last five years since Felix left, Poindexter wakes up at 2 a.m. and sits by the front door until daybreak, still waiting for Felix to come home.

I advise that if you have the opportunity to have all your animals present during your animal's passing and/or euthanasia, please take advantage of it. They need to be there to help comfort each other and to see their beloved brother, sister, friend, or mate transition. If this is not possible, please let them say goodbye before their physical separation, if you have the time. Their healing journey is not unlike ours, so be aware of this and help them understand what has happened.

After the loss of their companion, your animals may seem lethargic and/or distant for a while. When you feel the time is right, start to take them out again. Socialize them with other animals outside the house, and also have playdates at your home whenever possible. Always try to maintain their daily routine, no matter how hard—just one step at a time, one day at a time, as you keep moving forward. All animals like consistency and continuity, and maintaining their routine keeps them feeling safe during unstable times. As you watch your animals heal, let their healing resonate within you. Absorb any lessons that you can learn from watching them. Process their emotions as if they were your emotions, and know that all of you will be okay mending and moving forward together.

Moving Forward, Not Moving On

As you move forward in the healing process, it's natural to feel that your memory of your pet may be slipping away. You may begin to feel less upset or emotional about their loss. Please keep in mind that you are not forgetting your beloved animal, only viewing their loss in a different light. This is all positive, very natural, and therapeutic for healing. We both know that you will never forget their love, which you cherish so deeply. This shift in emotions is indicative of emotional growth. Settle with it and again acknowledge your progress.

Straight from the communicator's mouth: Moving forward doesn't take your pet's memory away. It allows you to permanently and deeply etch them in your heart forever.

Signs You Are Ready for a New Pet

Baby-stepping your way back into another pet's life is a great beginning for you and your new animal. There is no time frame for when you should take on a new family member. Let your little inner voice be your guide. So many of my clients have expressed that the new animal was the one who picked them instead of the other way around. Even if my clients weren't ready, they felt like the new animal was the best thing that ever happened to them. Let the cosmos be your guide; let it pick the right time for you.

The Adoption Process

Adopting or fostering can be an extremely rewarding process. For everyone who already has a rescue animal, what can I say— you already know this! I've been the CEO of a nonprofit 501(c)(3) horse and farm animal rescue since 2009. I can proudly say that we have rescued and rehomed more than 600 animals to date, so I do have a *little* experience with adopting and fostering!

For first-timers, the process can be easy to navigate. Let me help you with a few tips.

The first step is to clearly think about what type of animal will fit into your household. Take into consideration not only your personal lifestyle but also your present animals' routines. You may want to get a younger pet to help motivate your senior pet, or a senior pet may fit better into a less active lifestyle. When considering getting larger breeds or another large animal, such as a horse, other considerations arise. Make sure that you have their best interests in mind with what you can physically, emotionally, and most importantly, financially provide them.

After you have considered all these factors, go out and find your new partner! Working with your local shelters is always a great start, as you can "shop to adopt" online from home. Searching out a local rescue is helpful as well, but note that there may be a bit more paperwork and review involved if you adopt from a rescue. Don't take the extra scrutiny personally; I can assure you as a rescue CEO that it's only to protect the animal's welfare. Remember that these rescue animals have been abused or traumatized in one form or another in their past. The mission of every rescue is not just to rehome them but also to protect them in the future.

Volunteering

You can also consider volunteering at an animal shelter for a while. All animal shelters have a training program in place just for this. My local shelter even has a baby bottle program for animals that still need to be nursed but have lost their mothers. It can be highly rewarding to take on this challenge. Nothing better connects you to an animal like bottle-feeding a little angel back to health.

I was fortunate enough to bottle-feed my baby horse, Jasmine. It was the basis for our incredible connection, because she was just one hour old when I rescued her. Our bond has stayed strong her whole life, as she never forgot her tough beginning—born on a filthy feedlot, awaiting slaughter with her courageous mom, Princess.

So many of my clients start off by volunteering at shelters, enjoying their time getting to know the shelter animals and feeling the joy when they get adopted. Of course, the flip side is the pain when the animals get passed over time and time again. Every time I go to my local shelter to adopt (a.k.a. pull) a horse, I always come home with another animal—a dog, chicken, or rabbit, among others—because I just can't help myself. Being in the mix with all that energy can be a drain, but if you step in with a positive attitude, you will conquer the negativity and make a difference.

Fostering

Lastly, consider fostering a shelter animal until it can be properly adopted. However, be aware that you will probably fall in love with your foster animal and make them a permanent part of your family. That wouldn't be so bad, now would it?

Straight from the communicator's mouth: Saving one animal will not change the world, but surely for that one animal, the world will change forever.

Your Experience Can Help Others

Now that you are fully engaged in the healing process, let me suggest a few other avenues for your own growth and for the growth of others.

Consider joining one or more online pet loss support groups. I belong to many, and I see so many stories that will be familiar to all who have lost their animals. You will find like-minded people in these groups, which can be very helpful, as you can share your feelings and see that there are many steps along this healing path. You may also be able to help others who haven't progressed as far as you have by showing them compassion and letting them know you also feel their heartache.

I give lectures at my local pet cemetery for their own bereavement group. We discuss grief management and communicating with animals after they have passed on. Check your local neighborhood for support meet-up groups and see about joining one. If one is not available, maybe consider starting one of your own.

You have accepted your loss, and now you feel as though you are ready to talk about the afterlife, questioning where your animals go and what it is like. Let's open that channel as we begin our next chapter.

Three

QUESTIONS AND ANSWERS ABOUT PET AFTERLIFE

We commonly refer to an animal's transition from its physical body to the afterlife as "crossing the Rainbow Bridge." As its name implies, it is certainly a bridge from one dimension to another. I visit this alternate reality daily in my sessions, communicating with all kinds of animals whose spirits now reside across the Rainbow Bridge. In this chapter, we will give some context to this experience and discuss some common questions about this afterlife dimension.

The Rainbow Bridge

I feel that the most intimate time you can share with your animal is the moment when they transition over the Rainbow Bridge. Being asked to escort them across, preparing them for travel as the door opens to greet them, is the highest honor I can receive. I look at the "other side" as a parallel universe running next to ours in space and time. When the lines are blurred for that one split second, the animal's spirit moves across. I have helped thousands of animals in their passage, and for me, spending time across the Rainbow Bridge is a natural daily occurrence.

Let's discuss this alternate dimension while I answer some of the most common questions about this experience. You likely want to know if your pet will still be able to watch over you, protect you, and comfort you. I've included a few stories about my clients to help illustrate the answers to some of these questions.

Question: Does it hurt when they cross over?

No, it does not hurt the animal to cross over. When I escort an animal across, I'm actually inside their body, feeling everything that they experience. Crossing over is instantaneous—in one split second, they are here and then they are there. When the body dies, the soul is immediately released and moves on to another place and time. One physical sensation that takes over me time and time again is a tingling vibration, a feeling of electricity traveling through me as the energy inside their body is released.

I have shared many of the experiences I've had of crossing over with two of my dear friends who are also veterinarians. They each specialize in a different field: One works with large and exotic animals, and the other works with smaller animals, such as canines and felines. They have both been instrumental in helping me look at these crossings from a scientific point of view. They understand me, because we share some of the same emotions about the afterlife. We all need someone to talk with about these experiences, even professionals like me.

Question: Do they make new friends?

They do make all kinds of new friends, and sometimes they are reunited with animals from your family that have crossed over before. This will occasionally include previous pets that they had never met before crossing over. It's always so rewarding for me when I'm talking with a pet on the other side and this phenomenon occurs. Here is one adventure when a human client of mine experienced that.

We were in session when all of a sudden, another animal appeared. I described her physically to my client, and she shrieked with joy.

"That's Tulip, my most special heart animal," she said. "I had her when I was growing up. She was everything to me!"

It's a deep emotional release for all involved when this takes place, and an honor for me to be part of the encounter. It's a wonderful surprise to be in session and find that a pet from the past is now with their animal on the other side. It doesn't matter whether they had met before or lived together at the same time in our dimension. The human caregiver is the connector they shared, and now they are together in the after-life. How amazing is that?

Question: Will they come back to visit?

Yes! They visit quite frequently, because they miss you just as much as you miss them. Some visit every day, and some will also bring friends—old and new—with them.

One of my clients, Casey, lived with her pet dog, Jack, a very large, handsome Bullmastiff, for 12 years. In Jack's mind, he was the one who had raised Casey. She had lost her year-old baby girl, Holly, in an unfortunate accident. As a single teen mom, Casey already had many challenges to conquer, and adopting

Jack was the only thing in her life that gave her stability at the time. He was truly her emotional support animal.

As Jack got older, medical conditions arose, and he was diagnosed with stage 4 lymphoma. Casey's heart was broken. She and I had several sessions, and here is what Jack had to say to her:

"I have to go now, because the pain is just too much to bear, and Holly is waiting for me. I have to go and be with her now."

Not being privy to Casey's personal past, I said, "Casey, who is Holly?"

Casey broke down crying, telling me that Holly was the name of her child who had passed. We were both speechless, our eyes filling with tears simultaneously. Holly had come to visit Jack from the other side and was ready and waiting to escort him over. Jack told Casey that she "was all grown up now"—a young, strong, and capable woman—and his job here was complete. His new mission awaited him on the other side with Holly.

Question: Can they feel my presence?

When you're missing and thinking of your animal, they can always feel your presence. This experience is supported by the yin and the yang of the universe—the balance of life—where all things are interconnected and counterbalanced.

Your bond is never lost or diminished by time and distance, and in fact, I believe that the spiritual connection is deeper and more defined once the animal has crossed. All your other senses kick into high gear now that you are no longer able to be in physical contact with your pet. It certainly can be spiritually rewarding and take you to new plateaus with your beloved animal, as their soul (and ours) lives on for eternity.

Question: Can their spirit be stuck between dimensions?

I'm frequently asked if animals can get trapped between the two dimensions. I have never personally spoken with an animal that was stuck between two planes, and I feel that this concept is best left to the movies and other stories about ghostly spirits.

Question: Will they be waiting for me when it's my time to cross over?

Sometimes yes, but this is not always the case, because it's not a given that they will be chosen to be your personal escort across. Sometimes the universe has an alternate plan for you.

We all hope to be greeted by one of our beloved pets when it's our time. I have a client, Marilyn, whose husband, Jay, was terminally ill and bedridden for several years. His loyal cat, Reggie, was his emotional support animal who helped Jay through the daily pain of dealing with cancer. Unfortunately, they lost Reggie to feline infectious peritonitis (FIP). Losing

Reggie was clearly difficult for Jay, given the comfort Reggie brought him. We began having sessions with Reggie from the other side, and he was very aware of Jay's condition as it worsened.

Jay had asked Reggie to always be there for him in his heart. Reggie replied that he "would *always* be there for him" and that he would come get Jay when it was his time to pass on. A few months after our last group session, I received a call from Marilyn, Jay's wife, who wanted to let me know that Jay had passed away at home in bed with her by his side. Most importantly, she wanted to share with me that right before Jay died, something incredible happened. He sat up in bed, stretched his arms out in front of him, and called out Reggie's name. For a split second, Marilyn saw Reggie on the bed, right on top of Jay's chest. What a monumental moment to share.

Reggie had kept his promise to Jay to be there when he passed, and they are both happily living together again in spirit in the afterlife. This gave Marilyn such peace of mind and happiness, knowing that Reggie and Jay were reunited. I only wish that we all could experience such a beautiful moment when we are called to travel.

Animals will often reconnect with their biological animal family or their human caretakers. Once I open the door to the other side for my clients, we never know who will show up. If you worry about your pet being lonely, I can assure you they are not. Yes, they miss you terribly, but they are always with old and new friends, humans and animals alike. Don't ever feel that they have forgotten you. For the animals, being on the other side is a natural flow of their spirit living on. It's another chapter in another dimension where they exist and thrive.

Question: Can I still talk to my pets after they have been gone for several years?

Yes, you can. I will give you some tools to practice with later on in this book. The time spent away has no bearing on the ability to communicate with your pets. Occasionally in a session, a pet that a person may have forgotten about drops in to visit, bringing up such sweet memories of a pet that has been long gone. This can also help accelerate the healing process as you uncover a deeper emotional loss, both here and in the present.

Question: What language(s) do they speak?

Animals totally understand all languages. I have animal clients all over the world that speak many different languages. You may be wondering how that is possible. I'm not a linguistics scholar, so it's fortunate for me that when I hear them, their words are translated into English, my first language. I did experience a few times over the years when an animal spoke to me in a language other than English—one horse spoke in Spanish, and another one in French. I believe that was because I do understand a bit of both those languages. As the receiver, my mind converts these transmissions into something I can comprehend.

When I say I talk or speak with the animals, I'm actually hearing their voices. It's unique for an interspecies communicator to have this ability; for me, it's no different than when you and I are having a conversation in real time. So, when I say that a particular animal said this or that, I'm actually quoting them.

Question: How do animals look in the afterlife?

I'm often asked if animals look any different after they have crossed. Do understand that I'm viewing the animal's essence, energy, or spirit, so my mind will show me what they looked like here on Earth even though their bodies were left long ago. I may have never met or seen a picture of them, but I can describe them perfectly for their human, to confirm that we are talking directly to their animal. As I mention elsewhere in this chapter, the animal's physical form is fully healed when they cross over the Rainbow Bridge. They project their physical being to me as we connect. Try to see it like a hologram—your mind recognizes the image, yet your conscious mind knows it's not real in the physical sense.

My clients often wonder if their dogs have reverted back to a younger puppy version of themselves. I have never personally seen an animal revert back to a younger version. They appear to be the same age as when they departed from their physical form.

Question: Are they healed from previous physical afflictions?

We worry about those pets that suffered great pain, especially if they battled a debilitating disease before they crossed over. Are they healed now, after being so physically impaired?

I can say that when I see them, they are always 100 percent physically sound, with no impairments whatsoever. One of the first things that animals that have endured this suffering want to share with their human is that they are pain-free at last. This helps relieve their human of any remaining guilt of whether they did enough to care for their animal.

Question: Do they forgive us after they are gone?

I want to share this story with you about forgiveness. A few weeks ago, I had the pleasure of reading for a very special teenager named Kat. One of her birds, Rami, had recently passed away. Rami was a colorful Conure parrot and Kat's soul mate. Kat wanted to ask Rami if he was still upset with her. Puzzled, I asked her to explain.

Kat would let Rami fly free around the house, where there were many glass doors and windows that he would occasionally fly into. One day he was flying very close to the glass doors again, and Kat scolded him. This upset Rami very much, and Kat felt terrible. When she asked for forgiveness in our session, Rami responded by saying, "I forgive you. I just got really scared because I didn't know what I did wrong. Now I know that you were just trying to keep me safe. Sometimes I did fly like crazy around the house, and I'm sorry I upset you."

It was very calming for Kat to hear that Rami forgave her. She felt terrible for raising her voice to him just before he passed. Now, with that burden lifted, she could be more centered and clearer about managing his absence from her life.

Question: Do they know why they passed on?

Another burning question Kat had was if animals know why they passed on. Rami shared that he had passed from old age. Many times, the animals can express exactly what happened as well as they can. They re-create their passing step by step for me in our sessions, letting me physically feel the entire process. They also share details about the physical surroundings and situations that may have contributed to their passing, which often helps us piece the puzzle together and gain closure about what transpired.

Question: How do animals actually visit us?

Animals do come and visit us quite frequently. As discussed in chapter 5 on page 59, signs that your animal has visited you can include hearing them, feeling their physical presence, and sometimes seeing them appear for a split second in their physical form. So many of my clients constantly ask when they will visit, often urgently—and understandably—stating that they need to feel their pets here with them again. Your animal may actually be visiting you right now; you only need to be open to observe it.

Here is a mental picture you can envision to help you get started:

Let your thoughts be lucid. Visualize yourself as a single drop of water, and now immerse yourself into the ocean. You are separate, but you are also part of a much larger existence. Your animal is now pure energy that can move across time and space with no restrictions, just as their spirit, or essence, moved on to the other side.

Question: Do our animals still love us after they are gone?

Animals have told me stories of watching their humans in their daily routines, observing their previous caretakers while they mourn their loss in various ways. So many of the animals see this touching behavior from us as we struggle to cope, and they love that we are still so deeply connected to them.

Question: Do they still play with their toys?

You might wonder if your animal plays with or misses their toys, including their favorite blanket or bed. No, they do not miss these possessions at all. After crossing over, they begin a totally new adventure apart from their earthly belongings.

Question: What do they want me to do with their things?

Most animals will say to share their favorite toys or belongings with other animals, to give them away, or pass them on to their own animal friends that were left behind, either in the home or at a day care or shelter. Animals are generous and want to pass what they have left behind to other animals in need.

Question: Would adopting another pet be okay with my departed pet?

I can say with all honesty that I have always received a yes to this question from the other side. Most of the time, the animals will even urge their owners to make room in their hearts for another pet right away.

I talked with a feline named Link from over the Rainbow Bridge, who summed it up nicely in a statement to his owner, Frank, when he asked about adding a new pet to the family.

"The love that you have deep inside you for the animals needs to be shared. All the beautiful years you gave me were amazing. Now it's time to share them again with another animal in need. Don't keep it locked up inside; I want you to feel love again. Another animal out there needs you. Save them like you saved me."

This passionate plea from Link to his human has resonated with so many. I can't tell you how many times I have repeated his exact words.

Question: Will they still be watching over me and my other pets after they have gone?

Your pet who has passed on may have been your emotional support animal or a support animal to one of your other pets. They will continue to visit all the time, keeping an eye on you and your needs, present for you even if you can't always see them with the naked eye.

I have a client, Maxine, who had a blind horse named Willow. Willow's disability seemed to be a grave situation at first, so we decided to discuss it in session and talk openly about it with the other horses in the herd, making them aware of the dangers of her blindness.

Willow's best friend, Pokey, spoke up during this session and said, "I will be her eyes. I have two and I can certainly share one." I suggested that Pokey wear a bell so that Willow could hear him out in the pasture. This worked well for many years. As time passed, Pokey crossed over the Rainbow Bridge first. With Willow's guide horse gone, Maxine asked herself what to do to continue caring for Willow. We went back into session, and Pokey said that he "would continue to guide Willow," explaining that "their bond was so strong, distance would not matter."

Maxine was nervous to let Willow in the pasture without Pokey's physical presence. She forced herself, and to her surprise, it was as if nothing had changed: Pokey's spirit was right beside Willow, still nudging her, guiding her, and keeping her safe. Willow never again had a misstep or accident, and she lived a full life to the age of 32 before crossing over from old age.

I have seen this type of commitment span many different situations. Support animals will stay devoted to you and their animal counterparts. If you are familiar with the term "guardian angel," then I know you will agree that Pokey is a perfect example of one.

Four
WAYS TO KEEP YOUR PET PRESENT

In this chapter, we will discuss physical and spiritual ways to keep your pet present every day. Let's start this chapter off with a quick update on Lana and Monty.

On the morning of this writing, Lana shared a most extraordinary experience that she had yesterday. She saw a young dog tied up outside a store, waiting for his human. He was the same breed and color as Monty: a chocolate-brown German Short-haired Pointer. As Lana walked over to the dog to say hello, he went berserk. He lunged at her, jumping up on her chest, and started kissing her all over. In that moment she felt like she was physically connected to Monty once again. It was extraordinary.

Just then, the dog's human caretaker walked out looking stunned and said he was in shock, as he had never seen his dog react this way. The pup, named Spuds, was known to be very unfriendly, sometimes aggressive, and definitely not open to strangers. Lana stayed a bit longer as her new friend kept pulling at his leash, wanting to give her some more love. She was overjoyed and cherished this, as she honored Monty's memory in her interaction with Spuds. The next day in session, I asked Monty if he had sent this boy to Lana, and he said, "Yes, but of course!" Lana said that if she ever ran into Spuds again, she might just have to doggie-nap him and take him home forever.

It's so important to keep your animal present in your life after they have moved on. In my practice, clients share many different and creative ways to achieve this. This is a time for you to mend, but try not to spend too much time crying. I know you have to release the pain, but remember that your animal misses you as much as you miss them. Instead, focus on the joy, love, and happiness you shared. This will mean the most to your pet, who will be watching you from the other side and who won't want to see you suffering. All the activities that you shared with your pet can remain a heartwarming memory for both of you.

You may be thinking, "Candi, I just can't. It's just too hard to do these things again without them."

Well, all I can say is that it's all in your attitude. You can still be introspective, but now that you have accepted your loss, let's change up your daily experience. Your grieving time is passing, and it's time to reset your mind, attitude, and heart. Fill yourself up with all the happy times you shared together, immersing yourself in the love that you were so lucky to share. Go out today and use Lana and Monty as your afterlife role models.

Honor Your Routine

From across the Rainbow Bridge, the animals want us to continue to live life and enjoy a happy and fulfilled lifestyle. If you have other pets to attend to, this should make it a bit easier. Just remember to always think of your departed animal. Include them mentally and emotionally as you work through your daily tasks. Talk about them to your other pets and let them know that their lost companion will never be forgotten.

Other methods of keeping your companion present include going to the places where you used to play, such as a dog or human park, and meeting up with other caretakers there that you know. Talk about your pet and share their personal story. Laugh and play with the other animals and enjoy yourself. At the end of a hard day's work, sit outside on your porch or balcony where your companion used to lie next to you. Take out a good book to read and relax with it, feeling your companion right by your side. Listen to the music that you shared. Sing out loud the songs that you played to celebrate them.

Another effective way of keeping your pet who has recently passed in your daily life is to simply go out for a walk and take the same route you used to take with them. In a session from the other side, Monty asked Lana to please keep going out for their daily walks, and he would be walking beside her in spirit. Lana listened, and not only is she walking again, but she also joined a gym and has a trainer. Monty is very pleased, because he wants her to stay healthy and strong.

These acts will help you keep your pet present. They are very common in the recovery journey, so don't feel that you are crazy or weird for wanting to do any or all of the above. I share these stories with you so you will know that you are not alone.

Toys, Bowls, and Beds

Looking at your animal's possessions and wondering what to do with them can be a hard experience to navigate. There are no incorrect choices to be made here, and you should always do what you feel comfortable doing, but I will give you a few suggestions to help you along.

You may want to keep something that can be a keepsake for a memorial altar, such as a blanket, sweater, leash, collar, bowl, harness, or toy. Several of my clients like to sleep with a keepsake on or next to their pillow. It's common to refrain from washing the pet's sweater, blanket, or anything that still smells like them. Don't judge yourself; go ahead and smell them, because your olfactory senses can activate sweet memories, just as certain songs can instantly take you right back to a particular place and time.

Another option would be to donate these items, which would be a generous act of kindness. Sharing their possessions with less fortunate animals is a heartfelt way to honor your pet. Your local shelter is always in need of blankets, beds, towels, and unopened food and medical supplies. Get in touch with a local rescue organization and ask what they have on their current wish list. It's easy to just drive over and make your donation. You may have more to share than you realized, including things like that old cat tree or dog crate collecting dust in your garage.

If you have already sorted and donated these things but you would like to do more, let me suggest that you go shopping at your local pet and tack supply house, purchasing new items for whatever type of animal makes you feel good. Then take these lovely items and donate them in your pet's honor. As a small side bonus, you may also receive a tax-deductible donation receipt. If you are interested in receiving a tax credit, check before donating to see if the rescue organization is a state registered nonprofit 501(c)(3).

It's always touching to me when passed-on pets want the friends they left behind to enjoy their things. Their wishes are not unlike the wishes we humans make when writing out a will. One animal, a Toy Poodle named Mickey, asked that his favorite toy be shared with his siblings. His prized possession was a half-stuffed monkey doll. He never let anyone get near it. But after his passing, he was ready to pass it to his housemates who had always admired it.

When Remembering Is Too Much

You may feel overwhelmed occasionally when you come across your pet's picture, collar, or other items that remind you of them. This is completely normal, and you will soon see that your reactions will change. If you need to put some things away for a while, that's okay. In time, you will be able to look at those things with fresh eyes and less pain. Remember, there are no time constraints on the healing process.

What's Left Behind

When talking with passed-on animals about what they want their human caretaker to do with their remains, I find that the answers differ. Their feelings vary from caring about every detail to having no interest at all about what happens to their physical remains. Sometimes in session, they help their human pick out an urn or box for their ashes. Feel free to keep it simple; the container does not have to be fancy or overcomplicated.

I have a client, Nikki, who lost her beloved Yorkshire Terrier, Fanny. Nikki opted for cremation and was reviewing a brochure for options for the container. Nikki had her heart set on the most elaborate and expensive urn. It looked like a Fabergé egg, a deep royal blue with an intricate pattern outlined in 14 carat gold paint. When we talked to Fanny about this, she asked for "the plain silver box, that was all [she] wanted." Unbeknownst to Nikki, Fanny had been watching her as she read through the brochure. Nikki purchased the plain silver box, as Fanny requested, placing it on the fireplace mantle. Later on, Nikki bought a real Fabergé egg to place on top of it, fulfilling both their wishes.

Pets have even asked their owners to put their remains in items that they already have in the house. It comes as a sweet surprise that your favorite vase or keepsake box is also your pet's. So, when asking yourself the question of what to do with their remains, literally think outside the usual box.

If your animal is interred at a public cemetery, visit their burial site whenever possible. Bring flowers and spend some time talking with them about how your day went. Reflect on your relationship and the time spent here together.

If you have the land available, you may inter your animal on your property. This is common for people with ranches that have larger breeds, such as horses, donkeys, sheep, goats, and other farm animals.

However, interring your animal on your property can be a challenge if you decide to move in the future. If you do move, you may be torn, because your new path includes leaving your animal's remains behind. You certainly don't want to be disrespectful to your pet's memory. Some of my clients who are faced with this dilemma exhume the remains and transfer them carefully to their new home so that they can be buried once again at the new location. This may sound extreme for some, but for others, it's not even up for discussion. They feel the need to visit their pet's gravesite daily and having them at home is the only option. The gravesite is a very special and private place for them to reflect and reconnect.

Honoring Your Pet

Honoring your relationship with your passed-on pet by sharing your love with a new pet can be highly rewarding. I do understand, though, that adding a new family member at this time could be challenging for some, and I realize that you would have to deal with new and old emotions at the same time. Your pet was truly special and one of a kind, so how in the world could you ever find a replacement?

Let's talk it out, shall we? You have come this far, so let's push your progress along a bit further. It's common for me to hear in my practice that human caretakers don't want to feel as though they are replacing their pet with another, and I have a simple answer for them.

Each animal is unique and has no bearing on those before or after them. It's okay if you're partial to a specific breed and/ or color, and there is no need to feel guilty about wanting another pet of the same type. Even if the new pet you choose is exactly the same on the outside, it will surely be their own individual self on the inside. Just take a look at we humans—many of us have the same skin color, hair, and eyes, but not one of us is exactly the same. Trust me, I know: I have older twin sisters who are literally nothing alike!

Try housesitting for a friend or keeping their pet at your home while they are away. It's a nice gesture and a great way to get some much-needed fur baby time in. You could take your friend's pet with you and share the activities that you once enjoyed with your pet, as I described earlier in this chapter. For larger animals, offer to go to a rescue barn and walk, feed, groom, and give affection to their animals. Spend time sitting with them in their stall and read some poetry; my own horse loves it when I read her Maya Angelou. Larger animals need just as much care and love as their smaller counterparts.

Again, you are not replacing your pet's presence, only sharing the human–animal connection with another one. Missing out on sleeping with or waking up next to your pet is normal; we all experience these types of withdrawal. Whatever you do to mesh yourself again with the animal world is acceptable.

I once received a remarkable request from a dog who was rescued from the 2009 Hurricane Katrina disaster in Louisiana. Her name is Marigold, and she's a sweet German Shepherd. Marigold's story shows us that animals never forget when another animal is left behind. It can be just as heartbreaking for them as it is for us.

Marigold was left alone in her abandoned house for five days before she was rescued, which severely damaged her psyche and caused her to develop classic PTSD symptoms. Marigold's post-rescue human, Dolly, was unaware of her past; she rescued Marigold from Louisiana sight unseen and flew her directly to her home in California.

Dolly constantly asked Marigold in our sessions about what else she could do to make Marigold feel more secure when she's home alone. We worked for a while on Marigold's separation anxiety issues until one day we had a breakthrough. Marigold began telling me about a glass bowl with big bright blue rocks that had once sat on the coffee table in her old home, and I asked to have a closer look. Marigold then showed me a picture of a brilliant red-and-purple betta fish swimming in that bowl, who turned out to be Marigold's companion fish that had died in the storm. When Dolly heard this, she ran out that day to buy Marigold a new Betta fish companion, filled a large glass bowl with blue rocks, and set it on her coffee table.

Marigold was thrilled to have a finned companion again. We had a very happy ending, because this was the final touch to getting Marigold acclimated to her new home. Her attitude changed immediately, and she was able to spend the whole day alone without incident while Dolly was at work. Dolly shared with me that Marigold would sit and watch her Betta fish for hours, completely mesmerized and relaxed.

Who would have ever thought of those two as companions? Marigold is an example of how healing can take many forms.

The animals need to feel that they are still connected to their mates that have passed on. Their emotions are no different from ours; they mourn and grieve, too. Let them know that you see that they are hurting and that you acknowledge their pain. Healing together can make your bond that much stronger. Once we adopt these incredible animals into our hearts—whether two-legged, four-legged, winged, or finned—they look at us as their true family. Let them in as you recover and heal together. You just might find that their empathy runs so deep you can find total solace in it.

In the next chapter, we will discuss how to communicate with the spirit, here and beyond.

Five

COMMUNICATING WITH ANIMALS' SPIRITS

I believe everyone has the capacity to communicate with an animal's spirit. Humans and animals are all one universal mind, one tribe, and tapping into this ability can be an amazing, life-changing adventure. Everyone wants to know what his or her passed-on animal is thinking. The need to stay connected to them never fades and, in fact, it only gets stronger when we don't have their physical presence in our lives anymore. After our pets have left us, we want to see and/or feel some sign that they are still present and reaching out to us.

I want to start this chapter by sharing an intense encounter a client had when communicating with her cat across the Rainbow Bridge. I can honestly say that this is one of the most definitive and compelling examples I can share to date of spirit communication in our physical world.

Adrian desperately wanted a tangible sign from her beloved cat, Trooper, that he was visiting her. Trooper was a strong, loving, and handsome jet-black feline with intense green eyes. Adrian had meditated with candles since Trooper left, but her heart begged for more. She was desperately longing for a sign. I had worked with Adrian and her partner, Carlo, via Skype from their home in Italy. We shared a loving bond through their animals for many years, so I felt comfortable facilitating this difficult challenge for them.

We decided to set up a séance for Trooper in their cellar, which had brick walls and no windows or vents to the outside. The cellar was the perfect environment for such an experience—very calm and peaceful. I wanted Adrian to connect with Trooper this time without the assistance I gave in our previous sessions. I instructed her to go down to the cellar at daybreak and take Trooper's favorite orange candle. I told her to ask him to blow out the candle completely. This was to be done on her command and on a count of three.

Adrian lit the candle and began her meditation, invoking her vision and asking Trooper for this sign in our physical plane. Adrian told me that as she sat down, the room suddenly became very cold. She shook, not from the room's temperature but from within her body, down to her toes. As she lit the orange candle, she saw that her fingers had turned white. Then she began visualizing Trooper in her meditation, first seeing him overhead watching her, then coming down to sit beside her. Finally, she asked him to blow out the candle on her count.

Adrian's voice was cracking as she began the count to three. Her eyes filled up with tears and her heart filled with his love as she watched the flame quietly go out. In that moment, their two spirits meshed together, smudging all barriers of time and space. She will never forget that incredible experience for as long as she lives.

How to Communicate with Spirits

Because of the nature of my work, I'm lucky that I attract like-minded people in my life and my career. About 99 percent of my clients believe in interspecies communication, both here physically and in spirit. Occasionally, one will share with me that they are a bit skeptical, and my response to them also applies to this chapter. I explain that if they are unsure or otherwise "blocked," it will send a mixed message to their pet. If I'm sending out a telepathic invitation to talk, and my client is simultaneously sending out a message of apprehension, the animal can be confused by the crossed messages, which hampers the whole experience. After all, the client has been their caretaker and trusted companion.

If you are anxious, your pet's normal reaction is that something may be wrong. Once we get into our session, this apprehension changes rapidly as the client's animal reveals things that only the animal could have known. The human's veil of distrust lifts and the floodgates of communication burst open.

You don't need a purple velvet cape, crystal ball, or magical potions to succeed in communicating with the spirit. The ability to learn to connect with the universe comes from within you.

Let's talk about the importance of meditation, as I feel that it's the most basic component of communicating. I suggest learning to meditate and to make time for it at least twice each day. The ability to totally quiet your mind is a must. Eventually, this will become second nature and will allow you to flow easily into a meditative space whenever you choose. There are many different types of meditation modalities, so conduct a little research and pick the one that feels right for you. Place yourself in a calm state of emotion and meditate in a quiet physical space where you will be uninterrupted.

Open up your mind and let your thoughts ebb and flow. Then, start your breathing exercises, in through your nose and out through your mouth, counting to three on your inhalation and three again on your exhalation.

As you start to relax, you may find resistance throughout your body in the form of residual tension. Take a slow, deep breath in and then exhale as you relax each area of tension. Starting with your toes, continue this process all the way up your body to the top of your head, squeezing each area of tension as hard as you can and then releasing it as you move upward. Once you are in this relaxed state, ask your animal to come into your mind while keeping your eyes closed and relaxed. This is the place where your communication skills can flourish. This is where you meet your pet—this "middle space" between the two of you, deep inside your mind's eye, between here and beyond.

Consider interspecies communication as though we are all radio receivers. Some humans, like me, are born just a little bit more tuned in to this frequency. However, now it's your turn to dial it in and lock on. Your pet is always ready and willing to communicate with you, so don't be afraid to let it happen.

How Pets Are Different

Conversation with the spirit is not unlike the conversations we share daily with each other. Animals want to know what is new with the humans they left behind, and they often ask health-related questions as well. The main difference between communication with animals and with humans is simple: The animals are unfailingly honest and have no ego at all. The conversation can feel a little blunt at times, but it's always straight from the heart.

I'm so lucky and honored that I get to talk with all types of animals across the planet. These conversations always reflect the particular animal's personality. There are no guidelines on how a particular breed communicates differently from another, and each has their individual traits. I enjoy how funny the animals are; most of my sessions are joyous and filled with laughter. The animals have a very special way of making us humans look at ourselves, as they are pure and honest 100 percent of the time.

Reach Out

Your pets are already trying to communicate with you—you just need to be receptive to the signs. I will discuss various signs to look for in chapter 7 on page 97.

When you are connecting with a spirit, begin by opening the conversation with details about your day, catching up and talking as you normally would. Use this opportunity to tell your animal how you feel. There is no right or wrong way to start the conversation; just practice, practice, practice, and practice some more.

Ways You Might Feel Spirits

This section will discuss the most common ways that spirits transcend into our physical world. Although you long for this continued connection with your departed animal, you may find yourself questioning many things. Try to remain completely open and neutral while you open up to your sixth sense. Prepare to receive things that you will hear, feel, see, smell, taste, and dream in a new and vibrant light. There is no right or wrong way to accept the spirit into your world, so just relax and enjoy the new sensations.

Many of you are empaths or lightworkers and have just not realized it yet. I hope that as you work your way through this book you will gain personal confidence in this area.

Here are some examples of what you may encounter.

Hearing Them

Clairaudience means "clear-hearing," or the ability to hear an audio message from spirit. When the animals speak to me, it's just like you and I having a normal verbal conversation. Don't expect to hear a weird-sounding voice or one that is altered in any way. I find that most people experience hearing a message right as they wake up from a nap or sleep. Messages can be more easily received at such times because when your conscious mind is at rest, you are an open vessel. Once you have opened to this listening, you may also receive other audio transmissions from animal spirits, including hearing a gentle whisper in your ear when you least expect it.

Many of my clients have reported that they were just waking up when they suddenly heard their dog barking in the other room. At first they were shocked and thought that they were still dreaming, or that it was possibly the neighbor's pet that sounded like theirs. When the mind settled down after a few moments, they realized that it was truly their pet coming to say hello. Their pet wanted them to know that they were there, watching over them and reaching out to communicate.

Smelling Their Signature Scent

Clairalience means "clear-smelling," or the ability to smell things that are not in your present reality. You may have already experienced this with a departed human family member. You're just sitting at your desk working away, and suddenly you're overwhelmed by the recognizable fragrance of cigar smoke. You wonder if there is someone else in the house, until something in your mind clicks and reminds you that your Uncle Louie smoked cigars that smelled like that. Yes, he was visiting you in that very moment.

Clairalience applies to your animals in the same way. You could be relaxing and reading a book when out of nowhere you smell your pet as if he just came in from the rain outside. You look up toward the sky and know you just had a visitation from your pet.

We all have very strong pheromones that are unique to us. You miss your animal's scent in and around the house. You may have held on to your pet's blanket, sniffing it from time to time for comfort. Triggering such pleasant emotions is quite a normal practice, so stay open to these olfactory phenomena as you continue developing your sixth sense.

Tasting What They Taste

Clairgustance means "clear-tasting," or the ability to taste things that you are not currently eating. You could be standing at the kitchen counter preparing a salad when your mind shifts without permission and you suddenly taste chicken and rice—your passed-on pet's favorite meal. You then feel overwhelmed with emotion when you realize that this is the time of day you would be preparing your pet's dinner. You haven't bought any chicken since they crossed over, so you wonder how you could smell it. This was just a friendly visit from your animal, who was sharing their happy mealtime with you once again.

I experience clairgustance often when I'm in session and a client asks me what their pet's favorite food is. It makes it really easy for me to share the animal's likes and dislikes with their human caretaker. I've only had a few distasteful experiences—no pun intended—in my career. I was talking with a snake that had lost her appetite. When I asked what would motivate her to eat better, she let me taste her favorite meal—sadly, I got to taste a live rat!

Feeling Their Presence

Clairsentience means "clear-feeling." You are driving your car singing to the radio, feeling carefree, when out of nowhere you feel an overwhelming emotional message from your pet. Your first instinct may be that something is wrong. "Do they need me? Are they hurt?" Don't let these transmissions worry you, because they are always safe and happy on the other side.

Dig deeper and take a closer look at what you are feeling. Respect your animal's messages, as they may be reminiscing by sharing a past experience with you or just trying to con-nect with you today. Enjoy the message and add it to your spiritual palette; it's another way of connecting across the Rainbow Bridge.

Feeling Their Touch

Sometimes you can feel your pet's touch as if they are completely present, like physical beings again. They often connect with us by letting us feel their bodies close, right up against ours. You could get a lick on your face out of nowhere or a scratch on your arm as they look for attention.

My dog, Astro, who was a large Leonberger breed, presses up against my legs. He weighed much more than I do, so there is no mistaking his presence! It usually occurs when I'm folding laundry or doing mindless activities. Most of the time, when you establish a connection, your mind is far away from your pet. You're open and relaxed, sending out a perfect invitation for the spirit world to join you for a visit.

Spirit Orbs

Another component of spirit communication is seeing spirit orbs, which are usually seen as translucent circles. They can be viewed with the naked eye or appear in photographs, and they float freely around us in thin air. If you have never seen a spirit orb before, they are quite magnificent. They are semi-transparent, like soap bubbles, in shades of red, blue, green, and yellow—like the palette of the aurora borealis as it shifts and flows.

I believe that these orbs represent spirits' energies—either human or animal—in our present dimension. Sometimes the animals can see them when we can't. Don't be alarmed if they start showing up in your home; it is another peaceful sign of visitation from the other side. Quite often when clients send me a picture of a family gathering and comment that the only thing missing from the picture is their animal best friend, we take a closer look at the image and sometimes are lucky enough to find an orb floating around. This is not a spirit trapped between two worlds; it is just a visitor saying hello from another dimension.

Seeing Your Animal

You think you saw your pet appear in the living room today! I'm smiling as I write this, because this is one of the greatest gifts from the beyond. It's a remarkable feeling when you are fortunate enough to actually catch a glimpse of your animals. They appear just for a split second, and most of the time, they are semitransparent yet fully formed.

This type of sighting can also engage other senses, as does seeing another animal that reminds you of yours. For pets that live inside the house, the most common place for this vision is the bedroom, because it's a place of security and comfort, and the most time spent together is often at night and during sleep.

For my large animal friends, the most common place for a sighting is inside the barn. Hear your horses softly nicker at you, their hooves tapping on the ground, and their munching as they chew grass. Be ready and open to this exciting vision, know that you are one of the lucky ones, and take it all in, because sadly this vision will vanish just as quickly as it appeared.

Oversouling

I'm frequently asked about reincarnation, including the question whether your pet will return in another animal's form. You may have seen an animal that not only physically resembled your pet but spiritually as well. This happens quite often after a loss; you're trying to mesh your love with another animal that fits the bill. This is a natural way to feel, but again, no two animals are ever alike. When I go back and visit the same animals across the Rainbow Bridge—time and time again, year after year—their locations or companions may have changed, but they are still there. Their energy remains a free agent, physically unattached to any vessel.

Visions

Claircognizance means "clear-knowing," or the ability to know or experience something that you normally would have no previous knowledge of. There can be no logical explanation for it except that you just know it. As you open your third eye through meditation, you may experience seeing things when you are awake in a dreamlike state, or when you are actually dreaming.

Visions can come in many different forms, but it's up to you to decipher random thoughts firing off from true psychic visions. You may have already experienced a vision, such as picturing a friend you haven't seen in a while coming to visit. Then the next day, you get a call that this friend is right around the corner. Conscious rationalization has no place when dealing with your sixth sense. If you feel yourself mentally drifting into rationalization during a vision, cancel that trip.

Dreams

Dreaming about your animal is their way of reaching out. You may feel as though they are right there with you, sharing precious moments together again, and you wake up with a sense of fulfillment and love. This is the most common type of dream experience.

Quite often, I'm asked if a client's animal has a message for them. Of course they do; the animals want to stay close and in touch with us as much as we want to stay close and in touch with them. These lucid dreams can be very realistic. Besides just seeing your animal, you may feel them, smell them, and hear them. Here are some more examples of what to expect.

Common Signs in Dreams

What should you specifically look for in your dreams? Here are some of the most common visions and their meanings:

1. Recurring numbers: You may see numbers such as 22 or 11, also known as "angel numbers" (see page 100). This is your pet's way of telling you that they are here to protect and guide you.

2. Animal totems: Look carefully, because this is your personal animal totem that your pet has sent just for you.

3. White feathers: Your pet has gone through a positive transition. They are physically and emotionally healed.

4. Your passed-on animal's image: You and your animal continue to be spiritually connected.

5. Water: Your departed pet's soul has been cleansed, releasing all negativity that they once had in their life.

6. Cutting your hair: Your pet now feels unrestricted, they fit in easily, and they are comfortable with their surroundings.

7. Shopping: Your pet is centered, making new friends and trying out new things.

8. Freefalling: All confusion has left and your pet is lucid. For example, if they had dementia before, they are now relieved of this burden.

9. Dancing: This is your pet's expression of a joyful existence, sharing their love and passing it forward.

10. Eating: Your pet has an abundance of happiness. Their time in the afterlife is now their personal feast to enjoy.

Developing Your Intuition

Here are some simple and fun exercises to help you identify signs and develop your intuition.

Get together with a friend and gather up a plain deck of playing cards plus a piece of paper and a pen.

Now for the fun part: Start by slowly picking four cards at random. Decide on one feature to focus on—the color, suit, or number. Give the cards to your friend and ask them to choose one in their mind. Have them hold all four cards up with the backs of the cards facing you, and ask them to concentrate on the card they picked by sending you mental images of it.

Now it's your turn to touch the card that your partner chose. On the piece of paper, keep a record of how many times you do this and what your success rate is. You should see your score improve quickly over time. Besides using a deck of playing cards, you can also make up your own cards with varying colors and images. The basic idea is the same, no matter what you use to focus on. Start by practicing receiving telepathic messages from your friends in this way, and then move on to the animals. You will have a sense of when you have your psychic sea legs and you are ready for deeper waters.

When you feel comfortable taking on a more advanced challenge, have your friend bring their pet over for a visit. Begin by asking your friend, the caretaker, to quiz you on things that only they know the answers to, such as their animal's favorite food. Then ask the animal the same question.

Stay very open now—you may hear them speak, or they may show you a vision of the food, or you may actually taste it. Go for the first thing that enters your mind. Keep "score" the same way you did with the playing cards, and watch yourself expand your sixth sense.

This type of experience will flow naturally for you once you connect with the universe on this level. Remember to have fun with it, be patient, and don't rush. You are building up your paranormal muscles just like a bodybuilder. They don't achieve their physiques in just one day, and neither will you!

You may have more than one animal on the other side, and as you develop your intuition and reach out to them, you may wonder how you can tell the difference between them. You will easily be able to tell them apart, just as you could when they were physically here with you. I know that you have a separate sense of each of your animals, because no two are ever alike. Their physical appearance, how they moved about and carried their physical energy, their scent, and the way they made you feel spiritually in their presence all vary greatly from animal to animal. When you are focused on communicating with them, bring all these factors into your mind. When you're reunited through your communication, I promise you will be able to easily recognize each animal individually.

In the next chapter, we will dive even deeper into developing your animal communication skills. I will also share some simple rituals for you to practice and enjoy.

Six

RITUALS FOR REMEMBERING AND REACHING OUT

Rituals are another way of staying connected with our passed-on animals that can help us heal and grow spiritually. Physically doing something that connects you with your pet is nourishment for the soul, and in this chapter I share several ways to accomplish just that. This assortment of rituals can assist you in saying goodbye, dealing with a traumatic ending, or just wanting to be reunited. Look through the rituals and see which feel right to you. These are all positive affirmations, so no witchcraft or black magic is involved! If you don't have the specific items needed for a ritual, you can improvise with what you have, because these items only represent a physical form for the feelings that you put into them.

DAILY INTROSPECTIVE GROWTH MANTRA

Let's start off with this easy and introspective thought exercise, a daily mantra to keep you on a healthy track.

First, I want to give you a "Purple Heart." This is for your love and devotion to your animals.

You will begin by taking each letter of this Purple "HEART" and manifesting it into your life each day. Try reading it first thing in the morning to kick-start your day. Copy it down in a journal, on a piece of paper, or into an app on your phone, and take it with you when you're out and about. Read it when those waves of overwhelming emotion take over. Stop, go to a quiet place, and read it again and again. I'm sure it will be interesting to see how the meaning of the word "heart" changes for you as you travel through the grieving process. I have given you some starter words to begin with, but feel free to add your own interpretation.

H: Healing, Hopeful, Happy, Honored, Healthy

E: Evaluate, Emotions, Empathy, Elevate, Easy

A: Access, Admission, Attitude, Appreciation, Adaptability

R: Rainbow Bridge, Restore, Respect, Rejuvenate, Rapport

T: Truth, Time, Transition, Trust, Thankful

SPIRIT ANIMAL GUIDED RITUAL

This ritual provides an open door for whatever you would like to share with your animal. It's very helpful in all aspects of communication with them. Giving you a clear pathway to feel connected. Helping you cope with their transition. Dealing with your grief. Making amends after they are gone. Honoring them and showing your respect. The possibilities are up to you as you create your own personal incantation.

WHAT YOU WILL NEED

A flat surface on the ground to set up your ritual (preferably in nature)

A compass

4 stones or rocks of your choice; size does not matter

4 candles (1 dark green, 1 yellow, 1 blue, 1 red)

2 cups salt, or 8 feet string

Incense, a soothing fragrance of your choice

A picture or small keepsake from your beloved passed-on animal

1. Begin by taking out your compass and finding true North. Set up your 4 stones about 2 feet apart in a cross-like pattern, placing 1 stone in each direction (North, South, East, and West). Each geographic direction represents one of the four elements: North represents Earth, East represents Air, South represents Fire, and West represents Water.

2. Moving clockwise around your stones, place the dark green candle next to the North stone, the yellow candle next to the East stone, the red candle next to the South stone, and the blue candle next to the West stone.

3. Shake a circle of salt around the outside of the 4 stones. You can use the string to make the circle, if you prefer. Make sure there are no breaks in the circle.

4. Now, sitting inside the circle, place the incense and keepsake with you in the center of the stones. Light all 4 candles and the incense. Sit for a few minutes and meditate on what you want to achieve today through this communication ritual. When you are ready, open your eyes and proceed to the next step.

5. Using the chart at the bottom of the exercise, identify your spirit animal guide. Starting with the North, call on your guide by softly clapping your hands in a gentle rhythm, asking in your own words for the great animal of the North to appear. Now proceed in the same manner to the East, South, and West.

6. Feel the power of the stones around you as you connect with nature. Ask the great animal of the North, East, South, and West to help you mesh with the other great spirit animals. Now visualize your pet as if they're right there with you in the middle of the circle, and look deep into their eyes.

This process will open your third eye, and you may hear the animals speak to you. Engage with all four as they connect you with the elements of Earth, Air, Fire, and Water.

7. If you are not sure what to say to your pet, here are some thoughts: Let them know how much you love and miss them. Speak of what they meant to you. Ask for forgiveness if you have some residual guilt. Ask for guidance if you need to lean on them. Let them know that you will continue communication with them, and finally, ask them to send you a sign back.

8. Stop clapping and take it all in; smell the incense and feel the power you have invoked. Thank all four of your totems for their guidance and protection today. Thank the universe for opening up today and sharing them with you. Blow out the candles and extinguish the incense. You may want to keep this area sacred and only use it for ritual purposes in the future. Collect your stones and candles to use again and again.

Especially with this ritual, you will become more advanced as you use it. I'm only giving you a basic framework, and I don't want to feed you too much text on what to say or ask for. Let it flow from your heart. It can be different every time, as your communication needs change. You are crafting this ritual, so be creative and ask for what your heart tells you it needs.

ZODIAC SIGN	BIRTH DATE	SPIRIT ANIMAL GUIDE
AQUARIUS	JANUARY 20 TO FEBRUARY 18	OTTER
PISCES	FEBRUARY 19 TO MARCH 20	WOLF
ARIES	MARCH 21 TO APRIL 19	FALCON
TAURUS	APRIL 20 TO MAY 20	BEAVER
GEMINI	MAY 21 TO JUNE 20	DEER
CANCER	JUNE 21 TO JULY 21	WOODPECKER
LEO	JULY 22 TO AUGUST 21	SALMON
VIRGO	AUGUST 22 TO SEPTEMBER 21	BEAR
LIBRA	SEPTEMBER 22 TO OCTOBER 22	RAVEN
SCORPIO	OCTOBER 23 TO NOVEMBER 22	SNAKE
SAGITTARIUS	NOVEMBER 23 TO DECEMBER 21	OWL
CAPRICORN	DECEMBER 22 TO JANUARY 19	GOOSE

BEDTIME VISUALIZATION RITUAL

This ritual will help you connect with your pet time and time again and keep the channels open between you. The more you practice it, the easier it gets. This is a unique and beautiful way to unite with your animal on the other side. Many of my clients love this ritual and include it as part of their nightly bedtime routine.

WHAT YOU WILL NEED

Incense, a soothing fragrance of your choice

A personal keepsake that you feel connects you to your animal (e.g., a picture, your pet's collar, their blanket, toy, or name tag)

1 cup chamomile tea

A soft blanket

1. Light the incense and sit down on your bed.

2. When you feel ready, allow your mind to shift to thoughts of your beloved pet. Put your pet's keepsake(s) on your nightstand or next to you in bed. Engage the senses: Look at, hold, feel, and smell the items. Take a few sips of your tea as you start to relax.

3. Lie down on your back and cover yourself with your blanket. Close your eyes and uncross your hands and feet. Get comfortable. Feel your body sinking into your bed. Visualize your pet in your mind's eye as if you are together. You could

be playing in the park, hanging out watching TV, walking in the forest, or doing whatever comes to mind.

4. Now it's time to open up. Don't be afraid to let your emotions flow freely, as there is no right or wrong way to feel. You are safe here within yourself. You may feel tears of happiness or sadness wash over you. Connect with your pet as if they are actually with you right now, and drift into a twilight state, meshing your energy with your pet's.

5. When you wake up you will feel refreshed, centered, and settled.

COMMUNICATION RITUAL FOR QUESTIONS AND ANSWERS

This advanced ritual is very helpful to facilitate daily communication with your pet. You can do this ritual every day, but I suggest only once every 24 hours.

WHAT YOU WILL NEED

A safe place where you can relax and feel comfortable

A song that reminds you of your pet

A journal or piece of paper

A pen or pencil

1. In your safe place, start by playing a song that reminds you of your pet. Let your mind shift to thoughts of them, and begin to focus on what you want to say to them. This could be any of your unanswered questions for your pet—things you didn't get to ask them before they departed. Collect these thoughts and write them down in your journal or on a piece of paper. Make sure that you express each one of your questions in complete detail. When you're finished writing, read each one out loud. Set your journal down and lie down in your safe place.

2. Close your eyes and relax. Clear your mind and don't try to think about anything. Let your thoughts just flow in and flow out as you relax. Feel your body sinking into the bed as every muscle lets go of tension. Begin counting backward in twos from 100 down to 0—100, 98, 96, 94, and so on. Keep

counting down until your mind wanders and you naturally stop or fall asleep. You don't necessarily have to complete the countdown. When you are done, you may find that you have fallen totally asleep, or you're just lying there in a completely relaxed state. Distracting your conscious mind by counting backward allows your subconscious mind to capture your pet's thoughts and answers. It will now store them for you until your conscious mind is awake and ready to receive them.

3. When you wake up or feel that you are ready to open your eyes, the very first thing to do is pick up your journal. Start by reading your questions out loud one at a time. After you read each question, pause for a moment and pay attention to your subconscious mind as it speaks to you. Listen to the first response that comes into your mind and write it down. This will be your pet's direct response or answer to each of your questions. You will hear their response in your head speaking to you.

4. The most crucial part of this exercise is to immediately write down the answers you receive as soon as you open your eyes. Please do not do anything else before you start journaling. The flow of this connection has to be directly from your delta state of mind to consciousness.

COMMUNICATION RITUAL FOR
QUESTIONS AND ANSWERS CONTINUED

5. Keep your journal of questions and answers as a great resource when you need comfort or reassurance. Continuing this give-and-take with your pet without their physical presence is a meaningful gift you can give yourself with just a little practice.

DAILY RITUAL FOR REACHING OUT: THE MEMORIAL ALTAR

My client Sylvia gets great comfort from a memorial she created for her passed-on pet Archie, an adorable three-pound fawn-color Apple Head Chihuahua. You can easily create a memorial like Sylvia's for you and your pet with the items described below.

WHAT YOU WILL NEED

A personal space where you can sit or kneel

A table

Candles (my preferences are lavender, orange, and lemongrass)

Incense of choice (my preference is Nag Champa or jasmine)

A keepsake from your pet, such as their ashes (remains), collar, brush, toy, or a piece of their hair

Your favorite picture of your animal, framed and ready to stand up

1. Begin by finding a comfortable place in your home where you will be uninterrupted.

2. Set up your table in this area and place your items on it. Light the candles and incense. Take your pet's keepsake and place it on the altar. Place the picture of your pet at the memorial.

▶

3. Sit or kneel, centering yourself. Now is the time to relive your most cherished moments with your pet. As your memories make you cry and laugh, simply rejoice in the beautiful life you shared together.

Sylvia finds this practice so consoling, because she can visit this memorial whenever she misses Archie's presence. It helps fulfill her urge to be reunited with him, even in the wee hours of the morning.

YEARLY RITUAL FOR REMEMBRANCE

This is a very simple ritual that you can practice annually with your remaining animals on the special day of a passed-on pet's birth and/or passing.

WHAT YOU WILL NEED

A keepsake, such as your pet's collar, brush, sweater, or piece of their hair

1. For larger animals, take a piece of the hair that you saved from your departed pet and braid it into your remaining animals' hair. You can add a piece to your own hair as well. For smaller animals, you can take your passed-on pet's collar or sweater and place it on your remaining animals, or gently groom them with your passed-on pet's brush.

2. Use anything that has your passed-on pet's pheromones on it, and let your animals smell it as you tell stories to them about their lost mate.

3. As your animals' eyes close and they relax, visualize the good times that you shared living together as a family. Reminisce about what life was like, and tell stories of their time together. This special time will help your remaining pets to heal along with you.

Practicing this ritual every year will give you a tradition to cherish instead of dreading the memory of the day your

▶

companion was lost. As you learn to look forward to this yearly event, so will your other pets. You might even choose to wear their collar as a choker or place their ID tags on a chain and wear them like military dog tags. These practices will let your pets know you still care about their passed-on mates.

GRAVESITE RITUAL FOR REMEMBRANCE

A gravesite marker can be a more permanent symbol of your pet's existence. If they are buried in a pet cemetery, you may also consider purchasing a memorial bench or gazebo.

WHAT YOU WILL NEED

A physical marker of remembrance

Flowers or an offering, such as your pet's favorite treat

1. For this ritual you will need to take time out of your schedule to visit this grave marker. Make and follow a plan for your visit: Go as often as you feel necessary, bring flowers or any type of offering with you, and sit down and place your flowers or offering on the marker.

2. Make your pet's gravesite your personal and private sanctuary for remembrance.

3. Once you are there, begin your meditation process. Share your sweet memories together, and as you do so, visualize, feel, and taste them all. Dig deep to bring up your best and favorite adventures together.

MEMORIAL TATTOOS

Tattooing your passed-on animal onto your body is a permanent, lifelong memorial. First, you will need to spend time picking out the best picture of your pet for the tattoo design. You may already have the perfect one in mind, or this process may take a while as you sift through your options.

WHAT YOU WILL NEED

Your favorite photograph/image that depicts your animal's essence

A trustworthy tattoo artist

1. Once you choose the photo, the search begins for the perfect artist. Again, take your time and interview tattoo artists carefully. Once you feel comfortable with your choice, you can begin the drawing process. Spend a good amount of time discussing the design with your artist, particularly your pet's physical attributes and personality. This process alone can be very cathartic. Even if you ultimately choose not to complete the tattoo, you will have created an image that means the most to you, and you will always have it to remember your pet. Another option is to have the image made into a portrait.

2. Having the option to look at your pet on your skin every day and take them with you everywhere can give you a feeling of constant comfort. It's an absolute honor to wear

them proudly. My clients say that the best part of having a memorial tattoo is the reaction from other people. When people ask about the tattoo, you can share a little bit of your pet's story with a new friend, keeping your pet's energy alive and present.

As we move on, I will share advanced signs of communication from your passed-on pets, including how to identify them and what they mean.

Seven
SIGNS TO LOOK FOR

This chapter includes more examples of how our animals can connect with us. Animals are my jam, so this includes a detailed assortment of animal signs and sightings you may look for or have already experienced.

Signs from Beyond the Rainbow Bridge

One of the most common questions I receive is whether a specific feeling or experience is a sign from a pet from the afterlife. Indeed, most of the time, these signs and experiences are! Our pets love to let us know that they remain present and with us. As I shared previously, I feel that the afterlife is a parallel dimension to ours, and at certain times the lines between the dimensions blur, allowing the animals to appear in our realm of reality. Our pets will always come back to visit us. They love watching over us, as they assume the role of our guardian angel.

The distinctive thing about these phenomena is that they occur when we least expect them. They can occur at almost any time and take many forms. Don't ever be alarmed by such an event, as it is just your animals' way of reaching out to you and staying connected, positively and with love. Keep your eyes open; I'm always seeing new and creative ways that the animals reach out. I'll share a few of the most common experiences my clients have witnessed.

You could be sitting watching TV, cleaning up the dinner table, or walking into your bedroom when just for a split second, out of the corner of your eye, you see your pet standing there. They commonly look a bit transparent in these visitations, and you may also smell their scent.

When this happens, you may wonder if it's real or if you are just imagining it.

Lucky you! You just had a visitation from your pet from the afterlife. The more you relax into the idea of seeing your pet this way, the more receptive you will become to future experiences. Don't ever try to force it to happen, because that never works. Instead, stay open mentally so that when your pet does visit you will be able to maximize the experience and absorb every moment with all your senses.

Our animals often like to visit by pressing their body against ours, allowing them to feel their weight upon us again as they would in life. This includes leaning on our legs as we are standing, lying down on the pillow beside us at night, or cuddling up next to us on the couch. You may feel them in your lap as you are driving or brushing up against you as you take a walk. Or, as you sit down in your easy chair and reach down out of habit to pet your dog, you may still feel their presence beneath your fingertips.

I love it when my animals visit me like this. It's such a warm and welcome feeling to see and/or feel a beloved animal once again, even if it's for only a few moments. When this does occur to you, respond with welcoming love. Never fear it, because, again, it's your pet's way of being reunited with you, and it's a magical experience to see their physical image in front of you once again.

I suggest keeping a journal of these experiences, writing them down when they occur. Doing so will provide you with another way to keep your pet present in your life, allowing you to review your visitation experiences anytime you feel the need or desire.

Straight from the communicator's mouth: Just when you least expect it, the signs are everywhere.

Numbers

Some of the most common signs are recurring numbers and number patterns. They are also called "angel numbers," because they carry divine guidance, often occurring when a spirit is trying to contact you and show their presence. Your animal is now your guardian angel and wants to help you in your everyday life. Below, I have picked out two of my most commonly discussed number signs.

ANGEL NUMBER 11

You can be out and about doing your daily routine when you start to notice that you keep seeing the number 11. When you picked up your coffee at Starbucks, the clock on the wall was at 11 a.m. You picked up your lunch and the bill was $11.11. Later, you got a new work assignment that included reviewing 11 bullet points. Last but not least, before you went to bed you watched an episode of *Stranger Things*, but this time you focused on the girl named Eleven—the character with psychic abilities.

Eleven is the master number of intuition and is associated with introspection and empathy. Your animal is having you experience patterns of this number. The intention is to urge you to realize that now is the time for you to open up to your intuition, your sixth sense. Your animal feels that you are ready to elevate yourself spiritually and look at things that once were hidden from your conscious mind. No fear now as you move toward a new cosmic existence.

ANGEL NUMBER 22

Twenty-two is the master number of duality and is associated with a complete balance in life. You will be able to visualize anything you want to accomplish and then put these thoughts into reality. As a true leader, trailblazer, and pioneer filled only with positive intentions, you are capable of making your mark on the world during your journey here. The number 22 urges you to fulfill this aspect of you. The rough periods have passed and it's time to stabilize and center yourself from the inside. Stoke the fire inside you. Go out and make big changes for all as you lead by example.

One of my clients, Darlene, started seeing the number 22 every day after she lost her emotional support animal, a brown-and-white Holland Lop rabbit named Elliott, on February 22 (²⁄₂₂). Before Elliott's passing, he and Darlene were inseparable. Darlene was a military brat turned fashion designer, traveling the world for her career. Elliott was a trailblazer back when emotional support animals—especially rabbits—were uncommon. A favorite patron of the airline staff and a champion at flying first class, he traveled with Darlene to all her meetings and fashion shows.

On the day that Elliott departed, Darlene started a new sleep routine by going to bed much earlier than usual, at 10 p.m. sharp. As she fell asleep, her mind flashed on a military clock. Guess what? Ten p.m. is 2200 hours military time. The next day, the number 22 started showing up everywhere. Darlene filled her car with gas and the total charge was $22.00. She went to the dry cleaner and realized she had brought in 22 items. Looking over her sketches for an upcoming show, she had 22 dress designs. The number 22 was now a part of her life. Elliott continues to show Darlene he is still present, especially at night when she most needs the comfort of him being close.

Feathers

When you find a feather, it means that spirits are offering you love and harmony through guidance and support. If you are lucky enough to find a white feather, this is the ultimate sign of faith and protection. Typically, you will find two, three, or four feathers in just a few days. This means that spirits are trying to show you that this is a message for you alone and not a coincidence. Feel the love and comfort provided for you from beyond in this gift.

Animal Totems

Now that you are mentally open to receiving signs from spirits, you may see other signs that previously you did not notice. In this section, I'll explain what animal totem sightings mean and what they are trying to tell you.

You may be going about your normal day when you start seeing a particular animal everywhere. You notice them on billboards, commercials, packaging, clothing, jewelry, in dreams, and more. This is not a simple coincidence; through these sightings, your pet is trying to contact and guide you. Each animal has a particular meaning and message to share. Remember, the animals are showing themselves to provide guidance and support, never to hurt or harm you. Your spirit animal guide will help you navigate through challenging times in your life and bring enlightenment, vision, and love into your world.

I hope you enjoy learning about these animal totems as they bring you closer to understanding messages from the spirit world beyond.

THE BEAR

The Bear symbolizes stability, boundaries, and rebirth and brings innocence, purity, balance, and patience. It will show you that being quiet can be just as powerful as growling. Setting boundaries with others as you speak from your heart and learning to say no can be life-changing. You have nothing to fear as you approach life with power, grace, and integrity. You have the power of a bear; its perfect balance lies deep inside you.

Other attributes that the Bear brings are rebirth, empathy, reflection, and forgiveness. The Bear's presence shows you that being judgmental is a thing of the past. Criticism of others can sometimes reflect characteristics or habits you dislike in yourself. Letting your judgmental attitude slip away, you are now able to forgive all who have wronged you.

Lighten your load by emptying out that emotional trunk filled with criticism. Practice compassion over judgment and make this your daily mantra. Follow this message from the Bear.

THE CARDINAL

The Cardinal symbolizes balance, pleasure, and spirit, and finding the perfect level of spirituality in everyday physical pleasures. The word "cardinal" is derived from the Latin word *cardo*, meaning "axis" or "hinge." This signifies an open door for you between the spiritual and physical worlds.

Those of you who are already lightworkers can refocus in this dimension. Take time to reconnect with family and friends. Be passionate and show your love. The Cardinal also represents recuperation, recharging, and relaxation. This is a time to jump off the hamster wheel to find peace and get back into nature. Take time off and enjoy some quiet time alone. This applies to both your physical state and your emotional well-being.

We live in a very demanding time, always accessible by phone, email, messenger apps, and more. Turn all your devices off for a spell and just chill. Do whatever you enjoy, and most of all, don't feel guilty for doing it. We tend to jump from one project to another. Change up your routine now by making a new plan for a sweet and deserved break. I promise you that your performance level will rise. Recharge and feel energized as you move forward.

For those of you who have just begun your spiritual journeys, the Cardinal is one of the most powerful invitations you can receive. Don't delay; respond by mentally checking the box that you will be heeding the Cardinal's invitation to renewal. Follow this message from the Cardinal.

THE COYOTE

The Coyote symbolizes wisdom, intuition, and teamwork. Life is not always black and white, and with its ability to adapt to any environment, the Coyote can always find a balance somewhere in between.

Born with a deep intuitive nature, the Coyote can easily see through life's deceptions. On high alert 24/7, it is one step ahead of life's pitfalls by continuously crafting a safe environment as it moves from place to place. Always loyal, staying with his pack, the Coyote knows the value of family and shows us that so much more can be accomplished with a little help from our friends. The Coyote brings you tremendous psychic power as well by opening your third eye, allowing you to view things from a new level.

Your perspective on life may take a 180-degree turn when you spot the Coyote; you have opened up and you can't turn back. Relish these changes and trust that little voice in the back of your head, that sense in the pit of your stomach, knowing that you are right. Move forward and don't look back. You are now the spiritual warrior you once hoped to be. Follow this message from the Coyote.

THE CROW

The Crow symbolizes transformation, manifestation, and insight. For so long, the Crow has been associated with the darker side of things—a sign of impending doom or death. On the contrary, its heavy presence brings a time for big change.

In Native American folklore, the Crow has the ability to speak, making it one of the wisest birds. The Crow teaches you to defeat the roadblocks you have been stumbling over and helps you overcome self-sabotaging habitual behavior.

As the crow is attracted to all shiny things, you too can go after those jewels in life. Keep your eye on the prize and have the tenacity of the Crow under your wings. Follow this message from the Crow.

One of my clients, Kyra, lived at the top of Hollywood Hills, where she was accustomed to seeing some wildlife in her backyard—the occasional passing squirrel or coyote. Over the course of one week, she experienced sightings like never before.

One day, she was sunbathing with her eyes closed, relaxed and taking in the warmth of the day. Suddenly, she felt a presence and heard an unusual sound next to her. When she opened her eyes, a beautiful, big black crow was motionless on the lounge chair next to her, staring intensely at her. Kyra blinked several times to make sure she was not daydreaming. The crow remained next to her for only a few minutes before flying away, but to Kyra it felt more like an hour.

The next day, Kyra was up early on her way to yoga class. As she started her car, another crow came out of nowhere and landed on the hood. Her first instinct was to honk her horn at it, but a moment later, it walked right up to her windshield, settled, and stared at her through the glass, mesmerizing her once again. A few days later, Kyra walked her dogs to the local dog park for some fun. When they arrived, she sat on the bench to take a breather. As she looked to her right, another crow stood next to her in the grass.

What a week Kyra had, receiving such an intense barrage of spirit sightings. Looking back, she shared that something drastically changed inside her at that time. No doubt about it, the Crow is her spirit animal guide. Her house is now adorned with Crow decor. When new friends come over and inquire about her unique interior, Kyra loves to share her story about her encounters with the crows.

THE DOLPHIN

The Dolphin symbolizes happiness, intelligence, and protection. The Dolphin approach to life is filled with joy. They get along with all other species that surround them, showing us the way to be playful and kind and look for the good in everyone and everything.

Sailors consider dolphins a good luck omen and a positive sign from the universe. Through stories passed down over time, dolphins are known for being protective. It has been said that dolphins have rescued many humans from shark attacks and drowning. They are highly intelligent and connected with the flow of the universe. They also bring tranquility, calming and stabilizing the human spirit.

Overall, the Dolphin is one of the most identifiable animal spirits that we can relate to. When we see one, we typically smile and feel jubilant. The pleasure and delight that they bring to all is indescribable. Enjoy your Dolphin sighting and savor every moment. Follow the message from the Dolphin.

My friend Jewel spent the day at Zuma Beach enjoying nature with her friend and her kids. Jewel wasn't ever really into swimming in the ocean, but on this particular day, she was called to the sea. She jumped in, feeling a little apprehensive as the water rose around her, yet she also felt a sense of calm that pulled her in deeper. She started to swim beneath the surface, and the soothing water became clear and warm. As her fears of being in the water dissipated, she decided to be a bit more adventurous and swim out a bit farther. She dove down deeper, feeling the freedom of being weightless in the water. As she turned around to resurface, the most incredible thing happened: She found herself eye to eye with a dolphin, and they looked deeply into each other's souls. Jules felt connected with the whole universe during that moment.

I consider this a once-in-a-lifetime gift from the Dolphin. The experience has grounded Jules and given her clarity. Whenever she feels unsure or insecure about her presence, she remembers that we are all one universal mind. A drop of water in the sea of life.

THE GORILLA

The Gorilla symbolizes family, unity, and fairness. The importance of family is rooted deep in our souls. Upon sighting the Gorilla, reflect and revive family ties. Take extra time to make a call or stop in for a visit with your biological and nonbiological family, and the love you share with them can flourish. You can always make time for this if you put forth the effort.

Nurture this love of home and heart and bring it to its fullest potential. Your heart is one of the strongest muscles in your body, so don't be afraid to exercise it in beast mode.

The Gorilla also shows you your aptitude for fairness. Speak up for yourself and for others. Never be fearful of the repercussions of speaking the truth. Your strength is like no other and you will use it for the good of mankind.

The Gorilla also reflects independence, strength, and freedom, giving you permission to forgive yourself for past wrongdoings. Release your guilt and anger, no matter whose fault it was. Feel the power of the Gorilla allowing you to remember painful lessons that you will no longer dwell on, enabling you to free yourself. Take a leap into your future. Follow this message from the Gorilla.

THE HORSE

The Horse symbolizes freedom, respect, and duality. Whether you have ridden a horse or dreamed about riding one, the feeling of freedom is indescribable. Your departed animal has brought you the sign of the Horse to teach you that you can channel immense power with just the slightest touch.

Any good equestrian knows this balance of power within the horse. You can control their massive energy with just a touch of your finger on the reins or a slight press of your leg. The harder you pull, the harder they resist. To quote Sir Isaac Newton, "To every action there is always opposed an equal reaction." This balance lies in equal and opposite energies, aka yin and yang.

In his TED Talk "The Hidden Meanings of Yin and Yang," John Bellaimey describes the ancient Chinese "concept of dualism, describing how seemingly opposite or contrary forces may actually be complementary, interconnected, and interdependent in the natural world, and how they may give rise to each other as they interrelate to one another." The Horse, like yin and yang, brings this flexibility and give-and-take.

Absorb this special message and apply it to your life. In return, the universe will bring you freedom and love. Follow this message from the Horse.

THE LIZARD

The Lizard symbolizes healing, transitions, and visions. Let the Lizard take you on your own personal vision quest. Begin with your dreams, because the Lizard represents your spirit guide through the REM state and explores your dreams with intensity. They will vividly reveal things to you that your conscious mind was previously not aware of. Take notes, remembering every detail, no matter how small or insignificant it may seem. This is a time of transition and exploration for you. As you read back over your notes, try to visualize your dreams again as you manifest them into reality.

The Lizard also represents great psychic ability and healing power. Open up your third eye to all possibilities. You were born to help and heal others. You may have sensed this but chose to ignore the signs. Your healing energy will attract many people, so don't be alarmed, but feel the power surge inside and rise to the occasion. The sensation of spirit working through your hands will be life-changing for all concerned. Get involved with others when they need help, because your presence is always welcome. I suggest studying and developing your healing skills to share your gift. Many are in need of rejuvenating energy to heal their broken souls.

Today, the universe tells you it's go time. Follow this message from the Lizard.

THE OCTOPUS

The Octopus symbolizes flexibility, camouflage, and rebirth. It is a natural shape-shifter, changing its color whenever unsettled or disturbed. Upon sighting the Octopus, be flexible in trying different things in your life, such as a new wardrobe or hairstyle. See how you feel when bringing out different aspects of yourself, like an actor adapting to any new role. Enjoy and have fun experimenting with new, colorful versions of yourself. Remember that your genuine self is always at your center, so do not fear ever losing your core.

This is also a time to remove any negative people from your life, without revenge or malice. Step away from them and remove yourself from the relationship permanently. A positive trickle-down effect of the new you will help you reinvent yourself in all aspects of your being—physically, spiritually, emotionally, and mentally.

The Octopus also brings luck, joy, and fertility. This is a golden opportunity to manifest all good things in your life. Ask for abundance and chant your positive affirmations loud and clear, for they will be received and delivered. You are one with the universe at this particular moment in time. Follow this message from the Octopus.

THE PEACOCK

The Peacock symbolizes flamboyance, vanity, and elegance. Viewing this sign can be bittersweet, because it comes with a warning label. The eye on the peacock's tail feather is also associated with the evil eye. The evil eye was derived from the Arabic word *al-'ayn*, which simply means "the eye." Many wear the evil eye as jewelry or some other type of adornment to ward off evil spirits. A belief has been passed down over the years by storytellers that you can bring the evil eye's curse upon you through distasteful behavior, such as acts of selfishness, bragging, overindulgence, cruelty, judgment, pettiness, and narcissism. These can all be warning signs of impending doom.

On the flip side, this bird knows how to strut its stuff! The Peacock shows you the positive side of being in the forefront. If you have been hanging out in the wings, intimidated and introverted, now is the time to step onto center stage, shedding any fears or misgivings about who you really are. Be as proud as the Peacock, but always carry a sense of humility.

The Peacock also brings analysis and examination and asks you to look carefully at your path. Try to expand your vision beyond what is right in front of you. Think matters through to the end and be aware that there is more than what the naked eye can see. Read all contracts at least twice. Learn to rely on your reaction to the body language of others.

This is a great time to expand your psychic connection through visual analysis. With practice, you will be amazed by how easy people are to read. Let your conscious mind take over your emotional urges, desires, and reactions. Gain control and you will make better decisions from this day forward. Follow this message from the Peacock.

THE PORCUPINE

The Porcupine symbolizes curiosity, criticism, and intensity. It can look very intimidating from the outside while showing off its bouquet of quills. Be wary if you threaten the Porcupine, as it will attack you with great force, shooting out its quills in every direction with no regard for where they may land.

The Porcupine is extremely critical of others and judges everything about them, with words that can be just as sharp as its pointed barbs. Upon sighting the Porcupine, please learn to be mindful when you speak. Stop and count to three before you answer. Mind your own business and engage only when asked to participate. Your curiosity makes you want to join in, but learn to take a less critical approach and see where it leads you. Lean on your support team if necessary. Doing so doesn't make you weak. Rather, your stability and fortitude are some of your greatest qualities, and they usually land you right back in a leadership role.

The Porcupine also brings confidence and awareness. You are now capable of rising up from past mistakes, lifting the veil of darkness that has been in front of you. It will be easier to navigate around what once stumped you, feeling a sense of undeniable clarity and determination. Follow this message from the Porcupine.

The Porcupine's legs are short yet sturdy. Help it travel as many miles as necessary to reach your goals.

THE SPIDER

The Spider symbolizes creativity, artistry, and imagination. Upon sighting the Spider, let that bottled-up creative energy flow. Take a painting class, some singing lessons, guitar lessons, or dance classes, or start a manuscript—anything that sparks your creative interests. Take a chance and let your imagination run wild. Be totally open to things that you always dreamed of doing. You won't make a fool of yourself, I promise!

I personally encountered at least a dozen Black Widow spiders before I was asked to write this book. At first, I instinctively thought, "What in the world is bringing out all these creatures?" I quickly ushered them back outside where they would be safely away from my large dog's incisors. Later,

I thought about what I was missing creatively in my life. I have longed for a more substantial expression of my work, something more defined and permanent. And now here it is: this book. The Spider was showing me that my time had finally arrived, and I grabbed the opportunity. I know now that this book is the first in a series devoted to speaking up and out for the animals.

Think of the amazingly intricate webs the Spider spins. You have the same capabilities but in human form. Make a beautiful web for yourself and fill it with anything that makes your heart smile. Look around at the wonderful things before you, and know that you only have to pick one to start. Make the world a more colorful place by adding some of your sparkle to the universe. Follow this message from the Spider.

THE SQUIRREL

The Squirrel symbolizes resourcefulness, playfulness, and organization. Just think of how it gathers nuts and seeds, preparing for the winter and stowing them away until it digs them out to enjoy its harvest.

The Squirrel is also a little trickster who loves to tease and be a clown. However, we can learn a serious lesson. Thinking ahead can save you a lot of grief. Saving money for the slower times and having a financial cushion, for example, can give you a great feeling of security.

One of my clients, Joey, has a little squirrel in his backyard he named Rocky, who comes out every day to be hand-fed by Joey. Rocky also has a great time teasing Joey's dog, Frankie, a small white Shih Tzu. Rocky sits up in his tree and chatters away at Frankie, then comes down close for a sniff before scurrying right back up the tree. Frankie goes crazy with excitement and plays along, like a game of cat and mouse—or dog and squirrel. It's quite the concerto between the two of them.

I share this story because Joey had lost his previous dog, Jasper, a large black Lab, a while ago. Rocky would play the same games with him, too. When Jasper crossed over, Rocky was nowhere to be found, and Joey feared that something had happened to him. Once Frankie became a part of the family, though, Rocky reappeared and the daily shenanigans continued. Joey was overjoyed at Rocky's return. He shared with me that he felt close to Jasper through Rocky. His visits meant so much, and Joey is so grateful that Frankie can partake in little Rocky's antics now.

Be like the Squirrel, bright-eyed and bushy-tailed yet squirreling away your nuts for the future. Follow this message from the Squirrel.

THE STARFISH

The Starfish symbolizes protection, recovery, and regeneration. In folklore, it is believed that the Starfish can protect you from a broken heart. Many believe that wearing a starfish charm around your neck can bring you its protection.

The Starfish also has the astonishing power to regenerate an arm if one is damaged or broken off, a process that can take anywhere from a month up to a year. As long as their core, the central "disc," stays intact, forming a new limb is possible. We humans don't have this ability to form new body parts at will, but we do have the power to heal ourselves internally. Learn from your sighting of the Starfish that if you lose something, or you are broken, you can mend yourself.

To follow the sign of the Starfish, simply start by rebuilding your emotional and spiritual self from your core, just as it does. Reconstruct your thought patterns, so when you feel yourself slipping back into a negative cycle, make a change. Switch off your thoughts of impending doom and end the destructive, repetitive mental loop. Blaze a new path using the power of positive thinking. The more you travel on this new route, the faster you will see results. Eventually, the older negative pathways will atrophy and dissolve.

When you are faced with a situation that usually brings immediate distress, the distress will now be redirected. It will be wonderful to feel this change within you. I know you would agree that truly, you are the maker of your own destiny. Follow this message from the Starfish.

THE TORTOISE

The Tortoise symbolizes calmness, self-reliance, and consistency. The Tortoise is in the game for the long haul, showing determination and strength with every step it takes. It stays completely focused no matter how long it takes to reach its destination.

We are constantly being pulled here and there throughout our busy lives. As humans, we are not wired to sustain this constant pressure for too long. It chips away at our stability until we eventually crack and fall apart. The Tortoise is here to show you that it's time to re-center yourself, get grounded, and not let yourself get caught up in the drama of others.

I'm sure you can remember a situation where you were highly stressed. When you were finally able to leave it behind, however, your reaction seems almost ridiculous. How could that situation have affected you so adversely? Jumping into a swirling pot of anxiety can swallow you up, so take time out of your day to meditate, breathe, and become centered. Walk slowly but with confidence, like the Tortoise, and set a calmer pace for your life. It can bring abundance your way.

The Tortoise has been considered a good-luck charm to many for a long time. It moves slowly, focused and relaxed, reminding you to take your time. Find a quiet place to call your own—it can be just a corner in your house or apartment—and fill this area with things that make you smile. You may even want to place your altar to your animal here.

Allow yourself a certain amount of time every day to spend on reflection, meditation, and re-centering. Practice awareness of your spiritual well-being. Nurture it, respect it, and honor it. Follow this message from the Tortoise.

THE WOLF

The Wolf symbolizes courage, intuition, and strength. Sighting the Wolf means it's time to trust your intuition, because the Wolf brings you closer to your sixth sense. The Wolf is a defender, meeting things head-on. It does not practice the feeling of fear. It never takes time to question what it feels—it jumps in and takes action.

You may be in a situation that didn't turn out as planned, and that's okay—that's life. Tap into your memory bank and be confident that you can handle whatever comes your way. This is not your first rodeo, nor will it be your last. Upon sighting the Wolf, conjure up the strong warrior inside you. Walk tall, push your chest out, make yourself big, and take a stand. Be fierce and follow your gut.

The Wolf also displays speed, humor, and nimbleness. Put on your rose-colored glasses. Stop taking life so seriously and look at the funny side of it. Be agile and dodge despair and unhappiness. You have the ability to balance any situation and the speed to outrun any forecasted storm. Follow this message from the Wolf.

THE ZEBRA

The Zebra symbolizes friendship, guardianship, and individuality. Even though all zebras have stripes, no two have the same exact pattern. This is a perfect example of blending in while keeping one's individuality. The Zebra's stripes represent their earthly balance. Staying with the herd, protecting and watching one another, is a natural virtue.

Reach out to your friends or colleagues and set the same example. Collaborate on that project you have had your eye on and go for it. Put time aside for team building and interaction. Feel the excitement and power of a group effort. Uplift and motivate someone who needs a little boost.

You don't have to always do things by yourself. Practice connection with others, helping, educating, discovering, and nurturing. Let go of your doubts and join the herd, as it is waiting for you. Follow this message from the Zebra.

A Final Word: The Signs Are Everywhere

I hope that I have touched on a few signs of visitations from passed-on animals that you have personally experienced. My wish is to make you feel connected to the spirits now more than ever. Be aware that these signs are continuously happening all around you. These amazing messages sent from spirits are there to help you deal with everyday life in a more fruitful way. Healing you from across the Rainbow Bridge is only one of the gifts that the animals share with us. Remember all the memories, love, and devotion you share—and will continue to share—with your partner. Your heart animal will be with you forever and always.

In closing, I have one more story to share with you. I was in session this morning with one of my clients, June, and her dog Rosie, a stunning 11-year-old brown-and-beige female Shepherd mix. It had been a while since we last spoke, so we had a lot of new ground to cover as June caught me up. She had questions about signs from the universe she received in a dream. June lost her companion dog Marshall eight years earlier. At the time, she was adamant about her lack of interest in a new pet, feeling that she would never be ready to love an animal again. Then, June had a vision one night of a dog, a brown-and-beige female Shepherd, with its snout right up against her face. The dog was saying, "Please find me, please save me."

June woke up the next morning energized and determined to find this dog. She started looking at online rescue websites. When she logged on to the second one, *bam*! The very first picture featured an exact version of the dog in her dream. Her vision had manifested itself in reality, and the universe had set its course for June. A sign from her passed-on dog Marshall instructed her that it was time to open her heart once again. She went out that day to adopt Rosie and never looked back.

This is a lesson that teaches us all to roll with what life puts before us. We can make all the plans we want for our future, constructing very rigid schedules to follow, but the universe runs on its own timetable and has its own plans for each and every one of us. Let it be, go with the flow, and be open to life's mysteries here and beyond.

My hope is that I have shown you a clear and truer vision of the afterlife, opening up new avenues of actions and reactions. Your questions and deepest thoughts are shared by others who have also lost a loved one. The stories I have shared come directly from my experiences with my clients.

I'm right here, walking beside you toward the threshold. You see a door that calls to you and moves you toward it as if you are floating. Placing your hand on the crystal doorknob, you gently turn it to the right, pushing it forward as you lightly step outside. You look up, seeing the light ahead of you. Glancing at the doorway, you say a final goodbye to the house of pain.

Resources

Books

Blayney, R. A. *Transformation: Life Before Birth, Cosmic Consciousness and Alternate Realities* (Absent Publishing, 2018).

Browne, Sylvia. *All Pets Go to Heaven: The Spiritual Lives of the Animals We Love* (Touchstone, 2009).

Browne, Sylvia, Chris Dufresne, et al. *Animals on the Other Side*, 1st ed. (Angel Bea Publishing, 2005).

Browne, Sylvia. *Psychic: My Life in Two Worlds* (Harper One, 2010).

Fitzpatrick, Sonya. *There Are No Sad Dogs in Heaven: Finding Comfort After the Loss of a Pet* (New York: Berkley, 2013).

Goldenthal, Sara. *Tucker the Spirit Cat: A Meditation on Love and Hope for Anyone Grieving the Loss of an Animal Friend* (CreateSpace Independent Publishing Platform, 2011).

Jade, Serena. *Charismatic Connection: The Authentic Soul Mate Experience* (CreateSpace Independent Publishing Platform, 2012).

Katz, Jon. *Going Home: Finding Peace When Pets Die* (Villard, 2011).

Kircher, Melissa. *The Endless Story: Explaining Life and Death to Children* (CreateSpace Independent Publishing Platform, 2018).

Kurz, Gary. *Cold Noses at the Pearly Gates: A Book of Hope for Those Who Have Lost a Pet* (Citadel, 2008).

Kurz, Gary. *When Is Buddy Coming Home?: A Parent's Guide to Helping Your Child with the Loss of a Pet* (Citadel, 2017).

Ladwig, Dane. *Piercing the Veils of Death: A Paranormal Exploration* (CreateSpace Independent Publishing Platform, 2013).

de Lafayette, Maximillien. *Your Pets in the Afterlife: When Your Dead Pets Return to See You for the Last Time.* Times Square Press and Jami'va Ulema Ramadosh (New York, Cairo, Berlin: 2015).

Mellonie, Bryan and Robert Ingpen. *Lifetimes: The Beautiful Way to Explain Death to Children* (New York: Bantam, 1983).

Morita, Ken. *The World Between Lives 4: Real Testimonies of the Afterworld* (Zeus Publications, 2018).

Pepin, Eric J. *Silent Awakening: True Telepathy, Effective Energy Healing and the Journey to Infinite Awareness* (Higher Balance Publishing, 2013).

Shockley, David. *This Dog's Afterlife: Book 1* (CreateSpace Independent Publishing Platform, 2014).

Wintz, Jack. *I Will See You in Heaven* (Paraclete Press, 2018).

Websites

Association for Pet Loss and Bereavement: APLB.org

Candi Cane Cooper, Animal Communicator: CandiCaneCooper.com

The Humane Society of the United States: HumaneSociety.org

The Shelter Pet Project: TheShelterPetProject.org

Index

About the Author

 **Candi Cane Cooper** is an internationally acclaimed animal communicator who has been helping animals and humans all over the planet to coexist in harmony. One of her biggest honors is not only talking with animals beyond the Rainbow Bridge but also assisting them when it's their time to cross over. She was born with this gift and began talking with the animals when she was a small child. As Candi grew older, her desire to share her gift became overwhelming; it was time to come out and speak for those without a voice. The rest is history.

Candi has worked worldwide with thousands of clients for more than two decades. She is a devout vegan, living a compassionate, peaceful lifestyle. A native Californian, born and raised in West Hollywood, Candi currently resides in the San Fernando Valley with her two-legged life partner and all their beloved animals.